The Best of Solomon

Part 1

NOT PROOFED

Robert Mounce

ii

Dedicated to you,
the reader

Table of Contents

One

The summum bonum of life

The book of Proverbs was written, or in certain cases compiled, by king Solomon who ruled over the nation of Israel some 950 years before Christ. His wealth and wisdom resonate down through the halls of history, as does his sizeable collection of some 700 wives and 300 concubines. The answer to the conundrum of wisdom and wives is probably that very few people always put into practice everything they know. It is simply human nature but that doesn't make a true statement wrong.

Solomon begins his collection of proverbs by telling us with clarity why it is that he has set out on the project. Before all else, the purpose is that they might gain wisdom, have a clear understanding of the insights of the wise, and that this, in turn, will result in just and orderly lives (1:1-3) . The value of wisdom lies not in its intellectual astuteness but in its help in living a life that is satisfying and productive. Wisdom is "moral instruction" (NET). Of those who pay attention to the proverbs and put them into action it will be said that their lives are "honest, just, and fair" (TEV).

Having said that, let's look at the proverb itself as a guide for living. A proverb has several values. First, it is the summary of people's experience over a long period of time. It has been found to work better than any of its alternatives. In a democracy we hold that the people's opinion should be followed because, over all, it is superior to the limited experience of a single person – king, sage, or president. There is safety in numbers. Another thing about the proverb is that it is short, pithy and easy to remember. For example, that "haste makes waste" is hard to forget because it is short and we've all found from experience that it works out that way.

So, to have a firm grasp on what the human race has discovered up until now about the way to experience the *summum bonum* of life, look to the wise proverb, especially as recorded in holy writ. It will provide "disciplined insight (TEV) into doing what is "right and just and fair." Solomon's goal is to help people understand and apply those insights that make for the better life.

Two
Wisdom and the fear of the Lord

"The fear of the Lord is the beginning of knowledge, but fools despise wisdom and instruction" (Proverbs 1:7).

The book of Proverbs has to do with knowledge, not simply information. The role of the proverb is to take information and show in a crisp and effective way, how it relates to life. Solomon holds that there is but one entrance to real knowledge and that is "fear of the Lord." So important is this basic truth that the phrase is repeated fourteen times in his book of wise sayings.

But what does it mean to fear the Lord? Probably the best translation of the Hebrew term is "reverential awe." However, it captures a wide range of meaning going all the way from shrinking back in terror to drawing close in awe. (Alan Ross in the EBC). It is the controlling principle of knowledge, the entrance to true understanding. Put simply, it says, "to have knowledge, you must first have reverence for the Lord" (TEV). There is no other way. To fear the Lord is the direct opposite of living as a "fool" (mentioned 34 times in the book).

As we work our way through Proverbs, discussing four or five individual sayings in each chapter, we will be reminded of basic truths we probably have been aware of for a long time. What makes Proverbs so rewarding is that those same observations come into focus and become divine instruction on how to carry out our daily life. New life is breathed into ideas that earlier on did not impress us as being the mind of God. It is when we read a proverb as one who fears the Lord that we realize that God himself is the one speaking to us, helping us understand how best to meet the challenges of the day. God becomes our personal guide to understanding!

The second part of the verse speaks of the fool, one who has "no respect for wisdom and refuses to learn" (TEV). Solomon characterizes them as given to mocking (1:22), unwilling to accept good advice (10:8), immoral (10:18), always thinking they are right (12.15), unwise (14.13), proud (30:32), and on and on goes the negative description. It is an incredible privilege to realize that as we read and reflect on any one of Solomon's proverbs, God is there, wanting to teach us something of real value for life. Humility allows wisdom to be recognized and adopted, but the failure to stand in awe of God, who he is, what he has done, and what he says, blocks the path to genuine understanding. True knowledge is for those who stand in fear of the Lord.

Three

The self-destructive nature of desire

Have you ever wondered why the things we find most appealing often turn out to be so self-destructive? Read what Solomon has to say about greed.

"Such is the fate of all who are greedy for money; it robs them of life" (Proverbs 1:19 NLT).

To have at least a bit more, certainly describes the average person we meet – even when we look in the mirror. It may be more money, more prestige, more things, more time, whatever. It seems that having enough is not quite enough. That's simply human nature. We sometimes wish we could be more like the apostle who told the church in Philippi, "I have learned the secret of being content in any and every situation" (Phil. 4:11). That's a great goal, but let's stay with Proverbs 1:19 and the result of what the NIV calls "ill-gotten gain."

What strikes me is that we tend to be our own worst enemy. The things we desire the most often turn out to work against us. In today's proverb it is the desire for money. Many have found that a lifetime spent pursuing financial gain turns out to be far less satisfying than imagined. The dream house on the hill has been purchased but in the life long commitment to making it happen the family has fallen apart. As the quip puts it, "No man on his deathbed ever said, 'I wish I'd spent more time in the office.'" The intense desire to get what we told ourselves we had to have became our true enemy. It watched rather quizzically as those bent on achieving destroyed themself in the process. Such is the irony of life.

It is because what we want so often brings us down that God's way is always the best way. His "laws" (i.e., road signs warning us of dangers that lie ahead) are for our benefit. God has no desire to rob us of those things we hold to be justifiable pleasures of life, but he knows full well that if we allow our desire to change into greed it will destroy us. So Solomon warns us that an insatiable greed for riches is a sure road to disaster. Put more simply, "Greed robs a person of life."

Since that is true, as well as all the other "warnings" in scripture, ought we not to pursue a way of living that is devoid of all that appeals so strongly to our human nature? Since "God's way is always the best way" we can thank him for calling to our attention those pitfalls that appeal to our "old man?" Solomon's proverbs point out a way of living that protects us from self-destruction

Four
Wisdom won't speak until you stop

Solomon wants us to understand that as long as we are doing the talking, we can't hear what Wisdom would like to say.

Proverbs 1:21-23 is called "Wisdoms' Rebuke." It pictures

Wisdom calling out from the "top of the wall" and the "city gates" to the mockers and fools who refuse to listen to her advice. In vs. 23 she exhorts, "Repent at my rebuke" and adds that if they do, she will "pour out her thoughts" and "make them wise." Context describes the rebels as simple minded, unwilling to listen, and rejecting all correction. When disaster strikes and they call for help, God will "laugh" at them (v. 26) and leave them to "eat the bitter fruit of living their own way" (v. 31 NLT). Not a hopeful picture.

At the heart of their problem is an unwillingness – and to some extent their inability – to hear the clear voice of wisdom. They had ample time to listen and learn but they decided to do it their way. Richard (you wouldn't know him) was like that for some fifty years of his life. When God got him straightened out and I asked him what it was the brought about the change, he said, "My way wasn't working, so I tried God's way." In biblical language, he "repented," he turned 180 degrees and headed in the opposite direction. Solomon describes the result of such a change; it allows God to pour out his thoughts and make known his wisdom. It's important to realize that it is not up to us to somehow "gain" knowledge because God is ready to give it. The only thing that keeps us in the dark is our unwillingness to allow Wisdom to speak.

As long as we are doing the talking, enjoying center stage, we can't hear what God has to say. Enamored with our own insights it's difficult if not impossible to hear the truth. To repent is to realize our insignificance and step aside. God, who is eternal and omniscient, is the source of all wisdom. And the good news is that he wants to share it with us. By faith in Christ we become children of God and this relationship grants us contact with the source of all knowledge.

Five

Listen to Wisdom

"You simpletons rejected my advice when I warned you. As a result you must eat the bitter fruit of living your own way, choke on your own counsel" (Prov. 1:30-31).

One thing is crystal clear from the book of Proverbs and that is that actions have consequences. We understand that principle in the physical world – put your finger in a trap and, "Ouch! That hurts!" But we tend to forget that the same principle operates in other spheres as well.

Proverbs 1:20-31 describes how Wisdom responds to the various ways people treat her. One example is her reaction to "simpletons" (those who turn down wisdom and go their own way) who delight in mocking her. Verse 30 tells us what they do and verse 31 describes what happens as a result (and that' as sure as that sore finger you put in a trap not knowing it was set.) They "reject what wisdom has to tell them" (v. 30). They simply don't care what people have learned over the years about how life works.

When wisdom warns them what will happen if they do such and such, they do it anyway. God warns them but they couldn't care less. Why is that? In today's world it's because the "simpletons" believe that (1) all this god-talk belongs to a primitive culture that doesn't understand the advances in science, and (2) they know better than "god" – if there be one.

And what does Wisdom say about what will happen as a result? She says that they will "eat the fruit of their ways"(v. 30) that is, "they will get what they deserve"(TEV). Not only that, but they will "choke on their own schemes" (v. 31), "what they do will make them sick" (TEV). The consequence of not fearing the Lord but allowing natural desire to provide direction will end in something they will have earned but wish they hadn't.

One unique thing about sin is that it carries its own punishment. It is not that a person disobeys God and then God assigns a penalty. Result and cause are two parts of the same action. There are no causes without results and there are no results without corresponding causes. Wisdom understands this basic principle and directs us along the way. If we choose to pay no attention, then the wrong act itself exacts its payment. How good of Wisdom to point out the land mines along the path of life and give us a warning before we step on one. What happens in life depends upon our willingness to listen to what God has said.

Six

Knowing God

In Proverbs 2:1-6 Solomon is speaking of what it means to fear the Lord and to learn about God (v. 5). He gives his advice in a simple If-Then format – if you do this (vv. 1-4), then this will happen (v. 5). The If section states 8 conditions and is followed by a two-fold result. A quick read shows that the prerequisites for acquiring wisdom are:

Accept my words – *store up* my commands

Listen to wisdom – *concentrate on* understanding

Beg for knowledge – *plead for* insight

Seek it like silver – *search for* it like treasure

It is clear that the goal is not something that happens accidentally but requires considerable effort. Wisdom is not a free gift distributed somewhat carelessly to the uninvolved. When it is sought in the way described, the result is a deeper reverence for the Lord and an increased knowledge of God.

It is important to note that Wisdom is not so much to know about God as it is to experience him. Solomon is not laying out requirements for learning about the world in which we live, but the way to know the One who created it. Information is important and should not be dismissed as irrelevant, but the more important thing is to know God.

Christian thought assumes the existence of God, a spiritual being. To call that belief an assumption does not make God less likely. All worldviews begin with an assumption, even atheism (since it believes without support of any kind that God does not exist). Since God is a spiritual being our contact with him must be spiritual, that is, by means of the Spirit. The relevance of this is that knowing God, or learning how to fear him, is an experience made possible by his Spirit. Solomon is not teaching us how to be wiser in general but wiser in our relationship to God. That which we learn from textbooks may be informative and helpful, but it cannot help us arrive at wisdom in the way Solomon uses the word. The sage is telling us that to be wise (in the sense of an existential understanding of God who is spirit) we must genuinely desire wisdom and take the necessary steps to make it a reality. It is not that God

has a set of ironclad regulations we
have to meet but that we must
genuinely desire him to know him.
Ultimately that is the only kind of
"wisdom" that matters. As we read so
often in the OT, "The fear of the Lord
is the beginning of wisdom" (Psalm
11:10, Proverbs 1:7, 9:10).

Seven
Does God want us to be successful?

The basic point of Proverbs 2:1-6
is that if you search for wisdom as if it
were hidden treasure, you will come
to realize the awesome nature of God
and understand all that he has for you
to know. Then the rest of the chapter
speaks of four things that God in his

wisdom will give you. The first is "success" (NIV), and I put it in quotes because there is considerable discussion as to how the Hebrew word should be translated in this context: "help and protection (TEV)," "advice for the honest (NJB)," "a treasure of common sense (NLT)," "effective counsel (NET)."

Taking "success" in the normal sense of having accomplished one's goal, it seems at first to be a rather worldly objective for God to be concerned about. Why would he want us to acquire a profound understanding of who he is and what he does so that we can be successful in what we do? Feels like a spiritual method to achieve a non-spiritual objective. Does God want us to be successful in life? Well, he certainly wants us to be successful in our desire to live so as to bring honor to his name. But how does that relate to success in a profession or in the market place?

At the risk of sounding like a motivational speaker, I would argue that God wants each of us to be successful in whatever we set out to do. Why? Because a well performed secular act can be an expression of God's involvement in the life of the believer. It would be hard to argue that for a believer to carry out some daily task in an orderly and efficient way doesn't say something about their values. Who we are is clearly seen in what we do. Certainly this leaves no space for a poorly executed task. I believe that God wants each of us to carry out what we do in the most effective manner, for this reflects to a degree what kind of a God he is.

Success should not be limited to how the world usually understands it. It is not simply a larger house, a promotion to an even higher position in the company, a wider recognition by prominent people. While these are not to be excluded, success is doing whatever you do in an effective manner. A weary and disheveled cowboy just in from the range is just as successful as a new college president whose morning shower has left him clean as a whistle. Both are successful if they carry out their responsibilities effectively. For one, the calves that had strayed are back in the pasture; for the other, a good decision has been made regarding future direction of the institution. If both are believers their "success" in life is not unrelated to their relationship to God.

Eight
The benefits of wisdom

Wisdom is insight into consequences. It points out the right path and encourages you to take it. Read what Solomon has to say about it in Proverbs 2.9-11.

In our last conversation with Solomon he pointed out that one of the benefits of wisdom is success. Now he cites several more good things that will happen to those who embrace wisdom. First, they will understand the difference between right and wrong (v. 9). At the very heart of life is the moral obligation to do what we understand to be just and fair. Wisdom encourages us to be sensitive to this "oughtness" in life, which, in turn, helps to keep us on the path that leads to happiness. Secondly, we discover that wisdom is not merely external guidance, but it "will enter your heart" (v. 10). It helps one develop what in recent years is called emotional intelligence (EQ), the ability to recognize and manage one's emotions as a help in problem solving. To know something intellectually is helpful, but when wisdom "enters the heart" it is far more likely that something will be done about it. It is when information is internalized that we have the necessary stimulus for change.

A third result pointed out by Solomon is that when information is made relevant by personal involvement the person discovers that it is "pleasant to one's soul" (v. 10). It is unfortunate but true that in my own case the discovery of how exciting learning could be took place after, not before, my college education. Like it is for so many, learning was as bit of a chore instead of what it really is, a unique and exhilarating experience. My grandmother, who taught in a one room rural school for over 40 years, was convinced that heaven was the joyful privilege of being able to learn without interruption forever. I'm inclined to think those who might ask how that could be, haven't yet begun the wonderful journey.

And finally, with the entrance of wisdom, "discretion will protect" and "understanding will guard" (v. 11). As in the days of Solomon, so also today, the most effective way to remain safe is to understand and be aware of what it is that threatens and what can be done about it. On a material level this runs all the way from taking a sharp knife away from a child to heading to the shelter as the tornado approaches. But there are other kinds of dangers as well, such as the danger of a toxic ideology, an unrestrained life-style, an uninformed world-view. In every case wisdom will warn you that there is danger down this road. It is the rebel mind that chooses to stride ahead bravely ignoring the clear signs of danger. Wisdom is the close friend of all who prefer not to gamble with the one thing that cannot be replaced – time.

Nine
The crucial role of the parent.

"My child, if you store up in your heart and never forget all I've taught you about life, your days will be long and deeply satisfying" (Proverbs 3:1-2).

In these verses a father is encouraging his child to remember everything he has been taught so that the years that lie ahead will be profitable in every way. This will be the case only if the child remembers and puts into practice the lessons he has been taught. Throughout history the family has been the single most important factor in the stability and continuity of society. If God's plan for the family is set aside everything will be thrown into confusion. The more important lessons of life are best learned by a father's side or at a mother's knee. Remove that "classroom" and children are denied what they need most for a satisfying and productive life.

With the current changing of parental roles, it is yet to be seen what will result. It's good to see competent women filling vocational roles once held only by men. It is also encouraging to see men discovering the pleasure of an expanded involvement in the nurture of the young. However to redirect the traditional roles of the parent on anecdotal evidence is risky at best. God had something very clear in mind when he created man and women rather than some other combination.

Having said that, let's look quickly at some common goals in preparation for adulthood. As an evangelical Christian I would want my children to have healthy bodies, enjoy a rich family life, pursue a rewarding profession, and know God in an ever-deepening way. While others may have somewhat different goals for their children, the important thing, once goals are determined, is to discover the best ways to achieve them. And that is exactly what Solomon was talking about when he said to his child, "Store in your heart the lessons I've taught you." All through a child's formative years, the parent is pointing out the best way to accomplish specific tasks. What the parent now wants as their children move out on their own, is that what they have taught will be remembered.

I am convinced that effective character building is the finest gift any parent can give a child. This is the cooperative task of both father and mother. It demands time and energy. In a given case it may be possible to carry out this responsibility on a part-time basis, but time alone will display the validity of the principle. Should a parent ask why they should give such a large amount of time to a child, I would remind them that in addition to carrying out what is expected in a informed society, it is by giving that one receives. While we don't give in order to receive, we do experience the truth of Jesus' dictum, "If you lose your life for my sake" – and preparing a child for life fits into that category – "you will find it" (Matt. 16:25).

Ten
The answer is to trust

"Trust in the Lord with all your heart, not in what you understand from your limited perspective. Consult him about everything in life and keep you on the right path." (Proverbs 3:5-6)

We have come to a verse of scripture that is almost as well known as John 3:16. It would be hard to find a Christian adult who has not recited this verse to themselves again and again in a time of decision. Should I or should I not? Is this what God wants me to do? What about its impact on family? Then comes the verse and we hear God telling us to trust him completely in the decision. It's okay to think about the options but when push comes to shove don't trust your own insights. What you know is only part of the story; God knows the entire story and wants to help you make the right decision. And it doesn't matter whether that decision is really big and important or relatively mundane; he knows best. Our role is to "submit to him" (NIV) so he can direct our lives as he wishes.

I have the feeling that quite often when teaching a portion of scripture or using it for a sermon it would be best for the expositor to step aside and allow the reader to use the given time for personal meditation on the text. In the long run we really know only that which is revealed to us. Spiritual truth is personal and fulfills its purpose when it becomes active in a person's life. So I will stop here . . . or should I risk interfering with how God may be speaking to you through the above verses of scripture? Perhaps we may be able to achieve both.

I suspect that my decisions throughout life have not been much different than yours. When faced with the reality of sin and its penalty, I quickly headed down the aisle. I questioned where to go for higher education, what professional job I should take in life, who I should marriage, etc. As I look back there is one thing I can say with certainty and that is when I did what our passage for today says I found that the result was always good. And I mean always! But when I didn't listen, I got into trouble. Christian's agree that God's plan for life is the best, and the fact that we sometimes veer from this path simply validates the scriptural teaching that the old nature is flawed and wants us to repeat indefinitely the mistake of the Garden of Eden.

So let's reflect for a few moments on what God has to say about guidance in these two verses.

"Trust in the Lord with all your heart."

"Don't lean on your own understanding."

"Submit to Him in all your ways."

"He will keep you on the right path."

I'm glad you took my suggestion and if you jotted down what God said to you it would be interesting to compare notes – one sinner saved by grace to another.

Eleven
Receiving by giving

"Honor the Lord by taking some of the wealth you've gained and give it as a sacrifice to him. If you do, you'll have even more than you had" (Proverbs 3.9-10).

The original text speaks of the first fruits of a farmer's crop. To take from the first part of a harvest and give it to God as an offering was a way of acknowledging that the entire crop was provided by him. While "first" is temporal it also represents that which is best. In the two parallel clauses "first-fruits" is matched with "wealth." Since God created everything, all that is belongs to him and he should receive the first and best as an offering from those benefitted by his creative activity. When we honor him in this way he sees to it that our barns are full of grain and our wine vats overflow. Reduced to a formula it means that to give is to get. While that may sound a bit crass in some ears, and open to manipulation in others, it nevertheless is true. God is debtor to no man.

God would have us honor him with the recognition of who he is and all the he has done. That is exactly what happens when we take what we may have considered our own and present it to him. The problem in real life, however, is that most people, Christians included, tend to fail when it comes to honoring God in this way. We forget that every beat of our heart and every breath of air we breathe is provided by him for our benefit. To actively acknowledge his role in our "success" is the proper way for us to express our appreciation.

Generosity is a virtue highly regarded throughout the civilized world. Kahlil Gibra calls it "giving more than you can," and Richard Dawkins, the British evolutionary biologist, notes (in agreement with biblical teaching) that it's difficult "because we are born selfish." Almost every society admires the person who gives up something of personal benefit in order to use the time for a noble cause. Human nature has been marred by sin yet, when the stranger enters a burning building to save a mother's child, we honor his generous disregard for his life.

The result of generosity displayed in honoring the Lord with our wealth, all we have gathered as personal treasure, is that we become the benefactors of our own generosity. Our barns become full and wine vats begin to overflow. It was Francis of Assisi who coined the memorable dictum, "For it is in giving that we receive." And what we receive is not simply more of that which we gave but blessings of a different sort. To give a certain amount of money to a needy organization is not to get it back with a hearty interest but to realize, for example, that children in a war torn nation can survive today's horror and play and laugh again on a better tomorrow. Payment in kind is the cold exchange of the necessary. The true reward of generosity is the loving response of the one God allowed us to help by honoring him with whatever we have to give.

Twelve
The need for correction

"My child, don't turn a deaf ear when the Lord corrects you or resent the advice he gives because like our earthly father he corrects those he loves" (Proverbs 3.11-12).

It should not come as a surprise that the believer needs a certain amount of correction all along the way through life. We know that when we were growing up our fathers took time to show us how to handle the various challenges that arose. Whenever we failed to follow his advice he brought it to our attention. As adults we know that it is harder to give advice in an effective manner than to receive it.

Since that is true in normal family relationships, think how crucial it is in the spiritual. The only difference is that in the latter we have a Father who always does it in the best possible way. Very few, if any, of us would claim that in guiding our children along the right path we never failed to do it perfectly. The point is clear: loving involves correction, and hopefully it is given in the most effective manner.

To discipline those we love is a God-given responsibility. Looking back we can be glad for our parents' active concern for us. In wise and informed ways they taught us the necessity of diligence and the joy of accomplishment. For the rebellious among us the correction had to be a bit more stringent or it wouldn't have been effective. Hopefully the guidelines for conduct and the road to successful living were communicated with a minimum of unnecessary correction.

The fact that God actually loves us is remarkable. He, the perfect father, wants us to become his "perfect" children. He knows our natural inclinations and by the sacrifice of his Son, Jesus, paid the necessary price for our adoption back into his family. Now his love is active in helping us to accept his direction and be recognized as members of his family. We are to be living proof that sinners can become saints, that his Holy Spirit provides the necessary strength and guidance for our growth into Christian maturity.

Thirteen

Thee priceless value of wisdom

"Joyful are those who find wisdom because it's worth more than silver or gold" (Proverbs 3:13-14).

The book of Proverbs is an extended essay on the subject of wisdom. Of the 113 occurrences of the word in the OT more than forty percent are found in Proverbs. Solomon understands wisdom as the application of knowledge to life. If understanding is brain, wisdom is brain engaged with reality. Much has been written about knowledge and wisdom. Einstein reminds us that "any fool can know" but "the point is to understand." Socrates' famous maxim, "The unexamined life is not worth living" considers wisdom as one of the highest virtues. But what does Solomon writing under the inspiration of God's Holy Spirit, say about the value of wisdom? In today's proverb we learn that it is more profitable than silver and her yield is higher than gold. In short, wisdom is of greater value than anything else one could acquire.

The value we place on something reveals how important it is in our life. I happen to enjoy a good football game but there are those who literally live for football. The week is spent in anticipation of the next big game, making sure you don't misplace your tickets, and deciding whether or not to go to the hospital and have them check out that uneven heart beat lest they put you in bed. For a person like that, football has an enormous vale. Others would prefer a quiet afternoon reading and talking with their intellectual friends to driving umpteen miles to sit in crowded bleaches and root for the home team.

On the other hand there are those who seek wisdom, the deep rewarding experience of gaining insights into reality. Compared to that, a touchdown on "4th and goal" is rather drab. One person said, "Tell me what you pay attention to and I will tell you who you are." We create ourselves by what we think about and that can range from the tawdry to the sublime. In addition, wisdom is not only pleasant to grasp but it pays high dividends. Its rewards are more profitable than silver or gold.

It is sad but true that science accumulates knowledge faster than society gains wisdom. A major reason for international unrest right now is the tragic potential of nuclear weaponry. We should pray that society becomes wise in the benefits and power of nuclear energy before it simply wouldn't matter.

Fourteen
The art of translation

As many of you know, when it comes to the philosophy of translation there is a broad range of approach. One end of the spectrum looks for equivalent words in what is called the target language. At the other end, the concern is to make sure that what the author said in the source language is correctly represented in the target language. The word for word approach translates words while the other translates meaning. For instance, the ASV renders Proverbs 3:34 as, "*Surely he scoffeth at the scoffers; But he giveth grace unto the lowly.*" The Message translates the same verse with, "He gives proud skeptics a cold shoulder, but if you're down on your luck, he's right there to help." Some might ask, "But isn't the first a translation and the second a paraphrase?" The answer is a qualified Yes, but in a sense all translations are paraphrases because they all restate a given text in another language.

But some will ask, "Doesn't the word for word approach give you what the original text actually says?" My answer is that all translation involves interpretation. For instance, the ASV translates the first two words of Rom 3:4 with "God forbid" but neither

English word is in the Greek, *me genoito* ("not come into being"). The goal of all translation is to give the contemporary reader a correct understanding of what the original author wanted to communicate. The problem for the first approach is the non-literary result of handling words so mechanically. Words rarely have a single meaning that fits every possible context. As the noted linguist, Eugene Nida, insisted, "Words bleed their meaning from context." The question for the second approach with its freedom to select a right word in a given context is that the translator could, in the process, create what he would like the text to say. So while each approach has its challenges, both have a role to play when it comes to the art of translation.

With this in mind let's look at what

Solomon was saying in Proverbs 3:34. The NIV, probably the standard English translation right now, has as the subject of the verse "mocker." The ESV represents the original text as saying, "Toward the scorners he is scornful," while the TEV says, "He has no use for conceited people." Which is better – mocker, scorner, or conceited? As I hear it, "mocking" is rather specific ("to attack or treat with ridicule") while "conceit" is much broader. Which is better? To look for the answer the translator must go back into Solomon's culture with the Hebrew word, find out from the literature of the day how the word fell on the ears of those who first heard it. Would "mock," or perhaps some other synonym, represent to us today what the original meant to people then? But, you say, "Isn't that what scholars do?" and I would say, "Yes." Let's trust they have done the necessary research and let us hear the text as the first listeners did.

One thing is certain and that is that English translations are among the very best in the languages of the world. We can accept with confidence the work that continues to be done in the field. God will make sure that what He wants us to know will be adequately translated to all who desire to hear.

Fifteen
The benefits of wisdom
(Proverbs 4.4b-9)

The book of Proverbs has to do with wisdom, not knowledge in the sense of information about the world, but moral insight into life's deeper issues. Wisdom teaches us how to live so as to escape the follies of a thoughtless life and discover in our days the satisfaction of time well spent. Here in chapter 4 a father spells out to his son the benefits of acquiring wisdom. In verses 4b–11 are listed three of the most important with the first being life itself: "*Live by the principles I am teaching you and you will experience life as it is meant to be lived.*" Life is not the passing of time but our opportunity to experience in the deepest sense the rewards of living as God desires.

A second benefit of wisdom is protection, not simply from the dangers connected with living, but from missing out on all that could have been ours if we hadn't forgotten what we have learned (v. 6). Wisdom has a tendency to be overlooked when some immediate pleasure appears. Then in verses 7-9 we see that wisdom desires to honor us – *"Cherish her and she will exalt you; embrace her and she will bring you honor."* So, Solomon assures us that if we focus our energies on becoming wise (i.e., doing the right thing in every occasion) we will discover real life, be protected from all that would harm, and enjoy the honor justly given to the wise.

Well, that all sounds really good. Let's just learn from God and we will enjoy the benefits that follow. My question is, "Then why aren't we all wise?" I believe the answer is that wisdom is not that high a priority for most. The NIV translation of verse 7 is right on target: "The beginning of wisdom is this: Get wisdom!" The wisest thing a person can do is to determine to become wise. Wisdom isn't acquired by the passing of time or a laidback approach in the process. Wisdom begins by wanting it. "Though it cost you all you have," says the NIV, "get understanding." We admire the athlete who trains for years to compete in the Olympics, should we not put the same dedicated effort into living life as God intended, that is, becoming wise?" Wisdom begins by the desire to be wise and rewards us as we learned, with life, protection and honor. God's ways are inevitably the best.

Sixteen
How to differ, but wisely

One of the interesting things about Solomon's proverbs is that they are crystal clear. One need not wonder what the wise man meant when, for instance, in Proverbs he says, "Do not set foot on the path of the wicked" (4:14). We correctly understand that wicked people have a certain life-style and we are not to live that way. This is so important that Solomon restates it several times: *"Avoid it . . . don't even think about it . . . turn your back on it . . . keep moving"* (various translations of phrases in vv. 14-15). The wise man considers the way of the wicked and quickly decides against it.

But if our way of living is to be different from the life of the unbeliever, what about all of the acceptable things they do such as earning a living, raising a family, paying income tax? Don't we both live the same way in these areas? The answer, of course, is Yes. But what the proverb is talking about is the difference between a life governed by natural desires in contrast to a life lived in fellowship with God's Son. While there is common ground on a number of issues there is a distinct difference when it comes purpose and direction.

The point of the proverb is not that we should cut off contact with the world but that we should not become one with them. I remember from teaching World Religions that in every major religion separation from the wrong companions is essential for growth. Gautama Buddha wrote, "An insincere and evil friend is more to be feared than a wild beast; a wild beast may wound your body, but an evil friend will wound your mind." Those working with the data of sociology agree that people tend to unwittingly absorb the outlook and practices of those with whom whose they associate. No wonder Solomon warns against following "the path of evil doers" (NLT).

I know that the immediate reaction of some is, "But aren't we supposed to win people like that to Christ and how can we do that if we aren't together?"

To the two questions I would answer (1) Yes, and (2) Don't confuse normal contact with buddying. Christianity draws a clear line between good and evil. Spurgeon's response to the latter is, "If Christ has died for me, I cannot trifle with the evil that killed my best Friend." May God grant to each of us tender concern for the "not yets" of our community and a firm "no way" to a life style that placed our Lord on the cross.

Seventeen
The bright road of life

"The way of the righteous is like the sunrise, growing brighter and brighter until the full light of day has come. The way of the wicked, however, is like the deep darkness of night which brings down those who can't see the obstacle" (Proverbs 4:18).

In simplest terms, there are two ways the traveler can take through life. One way leads to an ever increasing brightness and the other to a fatal darkness. Why anyone would take the second path is hard to explain, but that they do is painfully clear. From a New Testament standpoint the righteous are those who by faith in Christ have been declared right with God. From that point on, life is a continuing experience of the bright light of confession becoming increasing brilliant as the believer moves toward the God who declared, "Let there be light, and there was light" (Gen. 1.3). The story of man can be pictured as a conflict between light and darkness. Light reveals God as its source, darkness as its enemy, and eternal brilliance as its goal. It speaks to the human heart with its message of hope and promise of guidance along the way. God is light.

On the other hand, darkness is the absence of light. When the primal pair left the Garden, burdened with shame, they stepped out of light and into a world of darkness. The first thing they did was to stumble. There is no pleasure in not being able to see. Goals are obscured and what might happen with the next step is unknown. The world without God is a vast sphere of darkness.

But Christ, the "light of the world," stepped into our dark domain and by his sacrificial life and death brought light back into this dark realm. What happened on a cosmic scale is repeated in a person's life as they turn from the darkness of sin and accept the light of the gospel. Each light grows brighter and as its light is shared with others everything becomes brighter and brighter. While we know that darkness continues its battle, the time will surely come when, as John puts it in his Revelation, "the eternal city needs neither sun nor moon because the glory of God is its light . . . and there will be no night there" (21:23, 25).

Two roads to walk: the road of light or the road of darkness. Solomon tells us that the second road leads to eternal darkness but the first to the eternal brilliance of his presence. The crucial difference between those who walk on one road or the other is whether they accept Christ, the light of the world who came to dispel the darkness of man's fatal mistake.

Eighteen
Do you understand our heart?

"Guard your heart before all else, because that's where your life is shaped" (Proverbs 4.23).

In biblical terminology the heart represents the center and source of a person's entire inner life, the seat of the will and its decisions, of moral life (both virtues and vices) and the direction it takes, and the emotions with their consequences (BDAG). The heart is at the very center of the influences that shape a destiny. One could say, "My heart is who I am." No wonder we are to guard it, and especially so since from the Garden it has a predilection to error.

What we do and what we say is simply an expression of who we are. If I respond vocally to some personal assault, it is my tongue doing what my heart tells it to do. Should I take advantage of someone when the opportunity presents itself, I am doing only what my heart recommends. Everything centers in the heart, so how misguided it is to attempt to correct an injustice by setting guidelines on what the body is allowed to do. The mind, emotions, and will are carrying out a response coming from the heart. Solutions happen when we deal with the "heart" of the matter, not the results.

So, it is reasonable to ask how we are to guard this heart, how to address the source of every difficulty. We might say, "My heart made me do it" but that won't work because the heart is precisely who we are. Our most effective counteractive method is to recognize our "prone to wander, Lord I feel it" nature and redirect our oversight so as to prevent what leads to our own total defeat. The crucial thing is that we understand who we are by nature, why we tend to say what we say, and how we are enabled by his Spirit to, as Solomon puts it, "guard our hearts." I believe the first and most important step is that we genuinely surrender to God; that means living moment by moment in a personal and authentic relationship to him. On one occasion I attended the little kirk near Balmoral and stood facing the royal pew singing God save the King/Queen in her presence. Enjoying God on a personal basis is like that unusual Scottish experience intensified beyond measure.

Nineteen
Be glad that God sees all

"The Lord sees everything you do, and gives consideration to your life choices" (Proverbs 5:21).

At Proverbs chapter 5 we come to a section that in most bibles carries a label such as "Warning against adultery" (NIV), or "Admonition to avoid seduction to evil" (NET), or as Dr. Schwab puts it a bit more graphically, "Advice about sex" (*Cornerstone Biblical Commentary*.) I once asked a widely known Old Testament authority whether, since Solomon had been dealing for 4 chapters with Wisdom, perhaps at this point he was not giving sexual advice but simply presenting Folly as an adulterous women. He gave me a quizzical look, but I still think that is an outside possibility. Since my choice of verses for comment is arbitrary, at this point I encourage you to read the chapter on your own. However, I will be commenting on the last three verse because they state so clearly three important lessons whether they are related to the preceding material or not.

There is no way to fool God. Our text declares that he "sees everything you do" (TEV). Taken at face value it pictures an all-seeing deity "spying" on his people. You may do your best to hide a sin but you can't escape his ever-present eye. Sort of gives most people the creeps. It's bad enough for modern technology to be able to see you through that little lens in your computer, or to track every email you've ever sent in order to build a case against you. But God has everyone of us under 24 hour scrutiny. At least that is one way some understand an omnipresent God. But let's consider his "seeing us" in a less negative sense. Perhaps he sees our intention in the act that turned out tragically wrong. He sees that what we did was born of love. Others may denounce us but God understands. Now, aren't you glad that you enjoy that level of helpful oversight? This understanding of the proverb is supported by the second clause, he gives consideration to the choices we have made. Not a spy with felonious intent but a paraclete resolved to help.

The question that arises for me is why it so easy to portray God as he isn't? Unfortunately, shame plays far too important a role in one's self-understanding. Each of us knows who we are by nature and it can be quite disturbing, but what about our perfection in Christ. There is nothing to be ashamed about when it comes to his transforming power. Any shame runs for cover when we rightly declare that God sees us as what we are becoming, not what we were. It's the devil who delights in making us miserable by cleverly leading us to think of ourselves as though in Christ the past were not over and gone. Scripture encourages us to live with the awareness that we are forgiven and that we are being transformed to look like the people we are in Christ.

So please examine me, God. I'm so glad I don't need to hide.

Twenty
The real problem of sinful acts

"The evil are trapped by their own sinful acts; they are caught in the net of their own sin" (Proverbs 5:22).

In a passage like this we should think of sin in personal terms. In this verse, picture the sinful act as a person laying out a trap for the unwary that happen to pass by. What we have is a spiritual civil war in which the sinful acts of a person become the sinners' own enemies. People sin and then find that they are caught in the net of their own actions.

A sinful act is not some isolated thing that a person does. It always has consequences. The act helps build an even more complex net that continues to entangle and imprison the sinner. We do it to ourselves. In a certain way we are our own worst enemy. I believe this is important and until we understand the deceptive nature of sin's opposition to righteousness there is little hope to escape its trap. For the uninformed, sin appears to be something they happen to do now and then. It is separate, without consequences, not something intrinsically involved in who we are. Granted, this is a gloomy subject, but until we discover the nature and source of sin we will never understand how it can be rendered impotent.

Here is the biblical picture. It began with Adam and Eve's decision to disobey God. The result was an alienation from God that became the determining factor in human nature. Created in God's image, but at odds with our Creator. As a result, history became an extended narrative on our propensity to act contrary to God will. It is not that people do things that are wrong, but that wrongness is part of who we are. Any attempt to formulate a righteous world is doomed to failure unless this point is understood. Society's answer is to correct what we do, while the right answer is to correct who we are. And that, of course, is where biblical truth is rightly understood as the only successful answer. God entered his own creation in the person of Jesus Christ. A perfect life was climaxed with a sacrificial death followed by a victorious resurrection. Now a righteous God announces to his wayward children that by faith they can return to that rich and rewarding relationship that was his intention for us. Nothing short of Spiritual renewal – and I capitalize the word because nothing but the Holy Spirit can provide the necessary power – can overcome our tendency to sin. Restoration and renewal is the result of taking God at his word.

We began with the picture of mankind ensnared by his native tendency to do what is wrong. I don't mean to say that people don't do good things, only that apart from God sin remains in control. The forces of evil allow us to appear to be on the bright side of life but, if Christian theology is correct, the world is infected by sin and only faith in Christ can offer the transforming power for recovery and renewal.

Twenty-one
Could we be our own enemy?

"Without self-control people die; they are led astray by their own stupidity" (Proverbs 5:23).

I believe it is crucial to understand that human nature lies at the root of every problem in life, whether personal or social. Most readers know the biblical account of Adam and Eve in the Garden of Eden, how they disobeyed God and were expelled. That separation from God left them with a flawed nature although they were made in God's image. Scripture teaches that this "old nature" is set against God and his righteousness and therefore in every decision will take the option that satisfies self. The Christian answer is that the eternal Son entered the world and by his sacrificial death gave those of faith a new nature with the power to defeat the desires of the person they once were.

And how does this relate to the proverb of today? For one thing it explains why people must be able to control themselves or they will die. To do whatever one might want in a world without boundaries sounds good to the "old man" and that "freedom" is exactly what a fallen nature wants. But, without protection of some sort the human nature destroys itself. It wasn't meant to be that way, but sin steered the human race off course.

Another point is that humanity's openness to be "led astray" is a display of its "stupidity" (TEV). It is not rational to live in a way that is detrimental to self. People do, but that's because what we want is stronger than what we know to be right. The apostle Paul talks about this in his letter to Rome where he confesses that he doesn't do what he wants to do but does do what he hates (7:15).

Solomon's proverb is not quite so theological as I have been discussing it and that's natural because with the coming of Christ and the ensuing testimony of New Testament teachers we have a better understanding of human nature and its effect on society as well as on the individual. Solomon, the sage, simply noticed that where self-control is lacking everything goes down hill and ultimately ends in death. Since the progression is not inevitable, the failure to make wise decisions is inescapable – it is "stupid."

Twenty-two
Proud that I have never "worked"

"Go and learn from the ant, you sluggard; watch how they live and you'll be smarter" (Proverbs 6:6).

Chapter 6 of Proverbs, like every other chapter in the book, has a lot to say about learning how to live. Solomon directs his barbs at those who have gotten into trouble in legal affairs, spent too much time sleeping rather than working, played the deceitful salesman, stirred up trouble in the community, or played footsy with his neighbors' wives. From this plethora of possibilities I'd like to discuss the lazy clod that needs to go and learn from the ant how to get organized and work. "Go learn from the ant" advises Solomon "and you'll find out how to live. "

They tell us that the ant has been around for a long long time. Probably that is why myrmecologists (I looked that one up) are able to identify over 12,000 different species. Unlike the human race they seem to accept the cold hard facts of life expectancy – drones may live only several weeks but the queen can last up to 30 years. They are famous for their work ethic and in the sonnet, *Of Ants and Men,* G. Ramel writes, "Who can believe the ants, they work so hard."

For many in today's world the word "work" has a rather heavy sound. It is what you do to have enough to live on. Real life begins "after work, or "after I retire." People go to the gym to "workout." A broken machine doesn't "work." But for many, "work" is an allotted period of time in which to accomplish what is expected. While I understand how the word "work" affects many, I would like to share a personal reaction to the subject. At 95 I have been involved in all sorts of work, including shocking wheat on a North Dakota farm, waxing the floors of a downtown Seattle haberdashery, selling vacuum cleaners door to door, serving our nation as a military pilot, teaching in a Christian college and serving as academic dean in a state university as well as president of a liberal arts university. So, in retirement, what have I been doing to fill the past 30 years? That's right, I've been "working" – published 6 books since bowing out of the work force). But for me, it has never been work (in the heavy sense). When you enjoy what you do, you don't "work" – you simply enjoy the place where God has placed you. Okay, in the beginning you may not look forward to what seems to be a menial thing, but certainly after college – if you go – you settle into what most call "your work." The neat thing is that if you enjoy what you do you never have to "work."

Remember when we used to sing, "Only one life, 'twill soon be past, only what's done for God will last?" True, but in addition to that higher calling there is a life that calls out to be lived. Show the world that the dingy concept of work is for those who for one reason or another haven't quite yet figured it out.

Twenty-three
Sand in the gears of life

In Proverbs 6:16-19 Solomon lists seven things that he simply will not tolerate; they are "detestable to him" (v. 16). We need to pay attention to the seriousness of this statement because God's concern is so great that words can hardly express his disgust. The first six form a group to which the seventh is added. Unless this six-plus-one is simply stylistic it places emphasis on last – "stirring up conflict." My plan is to list the first six and comment on the seventh.

Solomon begins his list of things the Lord hates with "haughty eyes," that is, the proud look of the arrogant. Second is the "lying tongue" – truth is so highly regarded that any deviation is an abomination. "Hands that shed innocent blood" refers to the customary manner in which people kill one another (some would hold that abortion belongs in this category.) God detests the "devising of wicked schemes" because it undermines the stability of family, civic group, or nation. "Feet that are quick to rush into evil" pictures the readiness of the rebel to break the established rules of society. And the first six end with God's abhorrence of lying under oath.

A terrible list of six malevolent practices, but there remains one more that is in a class by itself – "sirs up trouble in the community" (read family, friends, home-owners association, church, community, colleagues in any group.) It would appear that social turmoil is a condition that is unacceptable to God. God the creator set everything in motion in such a way that there would be a quiet efficiency i all the "running parts" of the universe – personal and in nature. You will remember that in the creation story, at the close of each day God surveyed his accomplishment and declared it "good" (Gen 1:4, 10, 12, etc.). But Paul, in Romans 8, pictures creation now groaning as in childbirth and waiting to be set right. And of course unrest exists everywhere in human hearts because

we tried in Adam to do it on our own
and the history of the human race has
turned out to be one of conflict and
dissension.

Well, that's the theology of it –
dissension is despised by God
because it affects everything
negatively. In the perfect plan
everything runs exactly as it should,
but when humans are factored in we
bring with us the sand and gravel of
our fallen nature and the giant gears
begin to groan and threaten to
collapse. Family life becomes more
tenuous, friends separate,
communities draw up battle lines, and
nations take up arms against one
another. Discord is a major force
working against God's plan and one in
which each of us by nature finds
ourselves.

May God grant us the strength of character to resist the temptation to "tell our side of the story," especially when the others probably will not listen anyway. Understanding, harmony, and goodwill should be characteristic of the various groups in which believers find themselves. It is how God planned it all.

Twenty-four
You've been warned, so Shape Up!

According to scripture, king Solomon had 700 wives and 300 concubines. Perhaps that makes him an expert on the subject dealt with in these 43 verses in Proverbs (6:20–7:27). It is summarized in 6:32, "The man who commits adultery is a fool because it's a sure way to destroy yourself."

The gist of the longer paragraph runs pretty much as follows:

"Remember what your father and mother taught you about having sex with another man's wife. She may be beautiful and seductive, but you'll pay a high price for sleeping with her. (You can hire a prostitute for a lot less and there's no risk.) It's like scooping fire into your lap. Should her husband come home unannounced and catch you in bed with her, you'll be in real trouble. You can't buy him off.

"Wisdom" is like your sister or aunt, so listen to what they have to say. They know how that questionable wife goes about her avocation. She leaves her house about sundown and

meanders down the street on the lookout for naive young men. She dresses like a prostitute so there'll be no question as to what she is about.

The simpleminded boy comes down the street and she takes ahold of him and gives him a kiss. Promising that her bed is fragrant and perfumed, she seduces him to go with her so they can "drink deeply of love till morning." Like a senseless ox on the way to slaughter, he believes her smooth talk about her husband being gone, thus leaving the bedroom safe until noon.

Wisdom would tell this simpleton that it will cost him everything he has, even his life. That loose-living wife is an accomplished seductress and the highway to death leads directly through her house. Her bedroom is the doorway to the chambers of death."

It is very clear that Solomon has given fair warning about the self-destructive nature of adultery. The unfaithful woman benefits in terms of the monetary nature of sex for hire, but el Dumbo has just paid for something that is ruining his own character. It is ironic that one's desire for sex outside of the marriage relationship carries such a high price. The $50 or so that one spends for the fling is nothing in comparison with the demands of a wounded conscience. Like all other sins, the unintended consequences are tremendous.

We live in a time of sexual exploitation for financial gain Companies utilize sex to sell everything from hamburgers to houses. Watch the next TV commercial to see how widespread is the practice. Society (including Christian society) needs to listen to Solomon on the subject. It's a very good idea to listen to Wisdom.

Twenty-five
The incredible value of wisdom

"This is Wisdom assuring you that my instruction is far better than gold or silver, even costly jewels. There is nothing comparable to the insight I provide" (Proverbs 8:10-11)

The entire book of Proverbs is full of wisdom. Nothing can compare with it. So why deal with the subject again? It's probably because it's so central to life. Today's summary statement (in 8:10-11) calls for attention. As every good teacher knows, "If their faces are still quizzical, say it again!" So, I will try to recap what we have learned about wisdom from Solomon.

One thing is for sure, it's more precious than anything you might possibly bring up. Should you stumble upon a hidden chest of gold and the genie gave you a choice between that treasure and wisdom, which would you choose? I know what you're thinking: With those resources I could hire the world's finest professional tutor in the subject and wouldn't that be "wiser?" Sounds like a good option, but since scripture is God speaking through Spirit-inspired intermediaries, wouldn't that be better? You'd be learning the "wisdom from heaven?" Since God is absolutely trustworthy and the wisdom he supplies is faultless, the better choice is the author of wisdom himself.

The traditional evangelical believes that scripture faithfully represents the mind of God. The words of Solomon, for example, are faultless. What he teaches is true by definition – he got it from the Source of all truth. So my is, why do we opt for something else now and then? And the answer is, that is what we are like as flawed images of God. What we often do is to set aside what God declares and go ahead with our own plans, and these vary according to today's political correctness. That is simply the way we are: We yield to what we want – its so appealing is it not? – rather than to what our Christian heritage affirms to be true

\What Solomon is saying is that we should follow the lead of Wisdom. She is an accomplished guide and assures us that her instruction is better, contrary to what we might think. Her instruction is better than gold, silver, or rubies. The wise among us agree, and play close attention to what she says.

Twenty-six
The tale of two women

"Does not wisdom call out? Does not understanding raise her voice?" (Proverbs 8:13).

In chapters 6 and 7 of Proverbs Solomon spoke extensively of the woman, Folly. Now in chapters 8 and

9 he speaks of lady, Wisdom. The contrast is as clear as it could possibly be. Folly is a wanton prostitute whose aim is to destroy; Wisdom is a beautiful and lovely lady who bestows rich benefits on those who seek her. One might call the two chapters, *The Tale of Two Women.*

The essay on Lady Wisdom begins with the important fact that she is looking for us, not the other way around. She "calls out!" she "raises her voice." She's on the look out for those who will listen to her and this is contrary to the idea that we are the ones doing our best to find her. The wise man is usually pictured as an elderly sort of monk who spends his time thinking deeply about the philosophical issues of life, hoping somehow to capture some new insight into reality. He is to be honored for reaching out to find truth, but truth seems to lie just beyond the fingertips of his mind. To this approach Solomon is saying, No, you've got it wrong. Wisdom is not hiding somewhere in the deep caverns of the mind but is there on the street corner calling out to anyone who will listen. If you have every been at Speakers' Corner in Hyde Park in London and watched the art of gaining and holding the attention of passer-byes, you get a good parallel for Wisdom a thousand years before Christ.

Once again, Wisdom is trying to get our attention, not the other way around. And why is that? Could it not be that if we are looking we are probably looking in the wrong places. Some are looking at ideologies that omit God as a basic premise. They do their best to understand such phenomena as the warlike nature of man, the answer to competing cultures, the failure to find meaning in a secular world. That's a challenging job; it leaves very little time for a person to sit back, relax, and ask if perhaps we are looking in the wrong place. In fact, they say, if the loud woman's voice I keep hearing would only be quiet I could do a better job trying to discover understanding. It's clear that if the befuddled person would simply listen and open up to learning the problem would be solved.

Wisdom seeks us. She wants us to understand the basic principles of life and is more than willing to teach if we will listen. On a practical level that means opening heart and mind to the existence of God. That is key. It provides the password to learning. It changes the strategy for achieving understanding. We need to quit our own proud attempts to learn by ourselves and allow God and his Spirit to lead us into truth. I can hear her call right now.

Twenty-seven
Does your church detest evil?

"Everyone who honors God for who he is will detest evil. As for me, I hate pride and arrogance, wicked behavior and corrupt speech" (Proverbs 8:13).

There is one thing you can say about Solomon and that is, he doesn't hold any punches. You want to know what he thinks? Just ask him and you'll get the answer. I'm not sure whether anyone asked him about the relationship between "honoring God" and "detesting evil," but his answer is that if you do the honoring it puts you immediately into the camp that detests evil.

Is that the way we find it in today's evangelical church? And by the "church" I mean real people who have come to Christ by faith and are relatively comfortable in the local assembly. It is so easy to talk about an organization and blur the fact that it is made up of real people, young and old, short and tall – the real people that make up the social unit. If I may express myself as John would, how much detesting of evil is there among the saints today? Yes, we detest various forms of the blatantly evil such as child molestation and mass murder but where should the line be drawn? How bad does evil have to be to be labeled evil? And who gets to draw the line?

I believe God hates evil with vehemence proportionate to his love of righteousness. Since this love is beyond measure, so also must be his hatred. I know that such a picture doesn't seem to be in sync with the God who is as revealed in Christ Jesus but perhaps our picture of Jesus has been photo-opted by contemporary religious culture. All I know is that Solomon, the sage, speaking for God, tells me that he "hates" evil because he "honors" God (the NIV choice of verbs). My point is that I, and I expect a lot of you, are a bit tepid in honoring and a bit too comfortable with its opposite. To detest evil is not to rant and rave about it, but to recognize it for what it is, and rule it off limits for life. But there is a better way to handle the problem and less liable to take us off course and that is to practice evil's opposite. The more we honor God for who he really is, the greater will grow our hatred of that which is diametrically opposed. I believe that as a nation we are entering a stage when men and women of faith will be compelled to take a stand.

With the rising surge of evil (all that stands over against godliness) there will no longer be a no-man's land where partial security may be found. Ideologies are increasingly separating our land and it follows that as the gap widens so also will the distance between the believer and the culture of this world. Yes, God loves them and has charged us with telling them the story, but from there on he takes over. Jesus reminds us that "if the world hates you, just remember that it has hated me first (John 15:18). Not a pleasant note on which to stop, but is it not also true that with separation from evil, the incredible joy of friendship with Him increases by proportionately?

Twenty-eight
How great, the love of God!

"I love those who love me, and whoever searches for me can find me" (Proverbs 8:17).

The first clause is a clear statement that God does not withhold his love from those who love him. In ancient days many tribes and cultures tended to believe that god was aloof and under no obligation to return favors to those who claimed him as their deity. To get god's approval required a significant effort on the part of the worshipper and even then it might not be enough or offered in an unacceptable way. The God of the Old Testament however, was a God who could be counted on to return the love offered by his chosen people. So Solomon makes it clear that God loved those who loved him.

Now in New Testament times one might question the same statement as not representing the God revealed in his Son, Christ Jesus. Didn't God say through John that he "loved the world" and that "whoever" believed would not perish (John 3:16)? That sounds like a pretty extensive and all-inclusive kind of love. Theologians will argue whether God's love can or cannot be considered "sufficient for all, efficient for some" but would it not be better to let it say what it says without undue concern for theological undertones? I know I am loved by God simply because I love him. My love doesn't make him love me; it is just a simple way to emphasize the mutuality of true love.

It is the second clause that reminds me that God is available for those who are serious about establishing a relationship with him. Those who "search" will "find." Here again, meaning can be diminished by losing focus in the pursuit of subtle nuances of meaning. Some might say, "But I thought that man, the sinner, doesn't search for God but spends his life trying to get away from him. Isn't

God the father of the prodigal son and in that role watches expectantly for the son to come to his senses and return home?" The answer is, Yes, God "searches" for us in the sense that he took the initiative and in the incarnate Son made a sacrifice that allowed all prodigal "sons" to return and be reunited with him. But in a slightly different sense, man "searches" for God. Deep in the heart of every person is a longing for something from without to come and fill the vacuum resulting from our being created in the image of God. That man is not aware of that which he longs for is but another aspect of the sinful nature.

So I would argue that God is searching for us and we are searching for him, although in different ways. To think seriously about the condition requires an openness to what all of scripture teaches and a willingness to accept the fact that language is a less than perfect instrument for transferring information. Rejoice in that fact that God loves you and however it happened, you are enabled to get what you really want.

Twenty-nine
Do you appreciate correction?

"If your correct mockers, they will hate you for it; but when you correct the wise it will be sincerely appreciated" (Proverbs 9:8).

Unless you feel you have to, it's not a good idea to correct another person. Normally all correction is considered criticism and at least part of the time you will be hated for your attempt to help. Solomon identifies the one who rejects correction as a mocker. However if the person you correct is wise, that person will respect you for what you have done. The lesson is that a person's character is demonstrated in how they respond to correction.

At one point in my theological training I was in a class in homiletics (preaching). Before the course was over, each student had to deliver a sermon to the class and then receive responses from the listeners. I remember one occasion when the student who was preaching was excessively nervous, so much so that the entire class felt ill at ease. My written comment was something like, "As one proclaiming the gospel you have no right to be nervous in the pulpit. It detracts from the message and makes it less effective." Years later I ran into him in a church where he served as assistant pastor. He took me aside and told me that my remark changed the entire way in which he went about the ministry. He accepted the fact that he had no right to reduce the effectiveness of a sermon by being nervous. It was a happy moment and made me wish I had been prayerfully corrective more often.

Why is it difficult to accept correction? Obviously because the corrector is, for whatever reason, saying that my performance was lacking. Now comes the interesting point – So . . . ? Shouldn't we be glad when someone points out a way in which our life-style could be enhanced? Yes, that is theoretically true, but we would rather not be reminded of our frailties and continue our happy life in Lala Land. Somehow we prefer to life as we always have in the sorry state of self-centeredness. We want people to admire us not correct us. But not the wise person. Wisdom is appreciative of suggestions as to how the task can be done better. They realize that mistakes can be a powerful tool for advancement. Just for the fun of it, the next time you blow it, how about swallowing any disappointment and praising God for the lesson you are learning. Granted, that is not natural, but are we not called to live supernatural lives?

Correct a mocker and he will hate you; correct a wise person and he will thank you for it.

Thirty
The irreplaceable nature of time

"Because of wisdom your days will be many and years will be added to your life" (Proverbs 9:11).

During the time in which Solomon wrote his proverbs it was widely assumed that there was a correlation between the way a person lived and how long they would live. I think that most of us would agree that in a broad sense the connection is still applicable. We would argue that the balanced life will outlast the rogue. However, apart from that probability I would like to consider other considerations related to the extension of life.

Life is good. It provides us with time to follow a profession that is not only rewarding in itself, but repays time spent with financial benefits that make creature comforts possible. If we hadn't been "on the job" today we never would have been able to eat at a nice restaurant, buy a new car, take a trip, etc. Time allows us to moderate our days with favorite pastimes such as gardening, music, reading, hiking, etc. But in what way does wisdom relate to all this? Good common sense (my definition of wisdom, rather than an advanced state of mental agility) encourages moderation in life style and that normally increases our number of years. So, live a normal life and you will probably have more years to do those things that make life here on earth more enjoyable.

That, having been said, I would like to suggest that there are ways to expand life regardless of its length. Watched a really good movie the other night, the South Korean documentary, "My love, don't cross that river." It chronicled the relatively short period before the couple's 76 years of marriage ended with his death. It was authentically honest, morally uplifting, beautifully done by Jin Mo-young, the filmmaker who, like a fly on the wall, was right there for last 15 months catching all the precious moments of true love. My point is that the experience of watching that film "expanded" the days of my life. Numerically my days remain the same, but realistically they were extended. Had I spend the same amount of time on some worthless activity (like watching weather on TV for umpteenth) my day would have been "shorter" to say nothing of being deprived of a meaningful involvement in the life of another.

Put it this way: wisdom will lengthen your days not only by giving you more of them, but also by allowing you to enrich them with all things worthwhile. The expansion of time is qualitative, not simply quantitative. Time being irreplaceable calls on the wise person to fill it with activities that bring the rich rewards of the brighter side of life.

Thirty-one
You can't get by with it

"*Stolen water is sweeter; stolen bread is more delicious*" (Proverbs 9.17).

Back in earlier days, "stealing watermelons" was a dangerous yet exhilarating experience. I was told – obviously it was the custom of other boys since I was such a pious young man – that there was nothing quite like it in the world; tasted scrumptious, the moon beamed its approval, and you had something to brag about. What is it that makes the unlawful so intriguing! There is no fun in washing dishes or going to bed on time. But if it's just a little bit naughty . . . that catches one's attention.

Everyone knows that if you cheat you'll probably get caught, if not now, then later. We know that if a person begins a little relationship with a neighbor's wife/husband they'll have to pay for it one way or another. The explanation for doing what is against one's own benefit lies in the garden story where the fruit on the forbidden tree looked so good. What would it hurt if they just tasted it? So they did and as surely as B follows A, result followed cause. God had told them not to eat of the tree. Satan suggested that God's advice was self-serving and argued that "stolen water is sweeter." So, of course, they took the exciting challenge and "stole" the fruit because isn't stolen fruit "more delicious?"

Mature believers know you can't put anything over on God. They've tried it many times but it has never worked out. Yet the appeal lingers and that is because the old nature lingers. Why is it that the Holy Spirit can't seem to control our fallen nature? Of course, he can, but we have to allow him. Sanctification continues at the rate we allow it. The problem is that in reality we tend to repeat the garden decision in so many ways. When tempted, we all too often respond on the basis of its appeal. Bad decision. Decide on the basis of what God has said (through scripture) plus common sense informed by his active presence though our conscience. Quit trying to resist it on your own; let God do it through his Spirit.

When I write on human nature I always feel a little down. It is genuinely too bad that Adam sinned. But there is also a bright side. God wants to use every testing period as an opportunity for growth into his likeness. He has an eternal banquet prepared for all those who would rather be with him than continue to "steal watermelons."

Thirty-two
The shut mouth: the secret of learning

"A sensible person is glad to receive instruction, but a numbskull who can't stop talking is headed for disaster"(Proverbs 10:8).

Solomon lays out a very simple test for determining whether a person is sensible or a numbskull. Of course, if we think we don't need any help in this area we have already placed our selves in the second group. The test is, Do they tend to listen or talk? When the name of John Doe comes up what is your immediate response? Is he given to talking or listening? Did you wonder whether he might be not to smart or that here was a person with insight? If you did what I suggested I am inclined to think that you came to a conclusion on that one. How could you help it?

The sensible person is glad to receive instruction. To learn what you did not know is far better than to tell others what could be new to you but old hat to them. I can see the look of incredulity spread across the their face as you begin to expound on the obvious. As a general rule, the sensible person has gotten to the place in their life that they realize that no matter how much they may have learned there is still the very real possibility that others may have gotten ahead of them in certain areas. Not only that, but the immature person engaged in discussion with others is liable to take the lead and tell everyone how much they have learned and can't seem to stop and find out what others knows. Proper balance is the goal.

One might ask about why certain people take over a conversation. I'm sure there are several reasons but one is that we are so involved in ours and love to talk about it that we assume on a practical level that others are equally interested. The root of every problem seems to be the self-centered nature of life. Just think for the moment how pleased you are when someone pays careful attention to what you are saying. It is satisfying to have others listen to and learn from what you are putting on the table.

The sensible person who gladly receives instruction is one who doesn't need the plaudits of some one else to feel they are of value. Down below the surface the talker is unsure of what he is saying. That's why he has to keep talking. The motivations for talking are many but most are unacceptable. Solomon knows that when a person is talking they are not listening or learning. The open mouth symbolizes a closed mind and that is why that kind of person is truthfully identified as numbskull. Sometimes when I am preparing a post for the day I wonder about which category I'm in. No one asked me to do what I am doing and it takes on average some 3-4 hours per day on a 7-day week with no vacation time. The answer is that I also intend to keep listening; listening to others who speak to the subject and especially to God who reminds me when I get off track. I've written over two million words and more are on their way. Incidentally, the bog has a

comment option so If you have a
response to anything I'd like to hear it.

Thirty-three
Was "victorious living" a
passing fad?

"*The mouth of the righteous is a
fountain of life, but the mouth of the
wicked hides a violent nature*"
(Proverbs 10:11).

I love that word picture – the
mouth of a righteous person as a
fountain from which life comes flowing
out. What a blessing to all within
earshot. Over time the body begins to
function a bit more slowly but the
heart can is ever new. However, all
along the line we needs refreshment

and how richly renewing are the wise words that keep coming from the mouth of the righteous.

I'd like to build a case today for what they used to call "victorious living" (1935 plus or minus a few years). The idea was that the Christian could (and should) maintain a certain buoyancy of life that demonstrated the incredible inner change of a person who would accept Christ as personal Savior. I'm quite sure that there were some authentic examples of complete victory over sin and life lived in the Spirit, but a candid appraisal of the group of which I was a member didn't have many who met the challenge. Where does one look to find a model for Christian living? When faced with that question most would begin to run through their years looking for those who fit the model –

always happy, big smiles, trouble free. But somehow the picture doesn't come into focus. Those who have been the most spiritually helpful to me are not the highly excited who have discovered the secret but the more thoughtful, just a bit laid back, and more thoughtful individuals. I find myself encouraged and challenged by being with them.

So perhaps "victorious living" is less a n emotional high as it is a deeper sense of belonging and relating to one another in the local worship center be it cathedral or front room. The limited "victories" I have experienced have left me somewhat quiet and appreciative of what God has done through my poor attempts to do it right. There is no flag raisings or Champaign to celebrate. Silence is beautiful in those moments of meaning growth in the Lord. I don't want to rush out and tell everyone of my victory on the front lines of God's special forces. I'm more apt to humbly thank him for his willingness to stay with me helping along the way until I become the person he sees in me.

A short way to make my point is to say that "Victory in Christ" need not by sung like a flamboyant cry of success but that "victory" rises from within in a surge of joy that leaves us humble before God and grateful for the moment. Spiritual "victory" leaves us aware of the quiet greatness of God, the remarkable power of his spirit within, and the desire to live more like the model that Jesus portrayed.

Back to the proverb, it is from this kind of victorious living there flows a "fountain of life." Super-saints are not performing on stage at the local church but living among us and sharing gladly with us what they are learning and experiencing in their walk with the Lord. They are the true "fountains of life."

Thirty-four
The atmosphere of heaven

"The prospect of the righteous is joy; but the expectations of the wicked come to nothing" (Proverbs 10:28).

Before we turn to the joy associated with righteousness and the disappointment that lies ahead for the wicked it will be helpful to identify the terms we are using. The proverb compares two kinds of people, the righteous and the wicked. In commenting on other proverbs I have defined the righteous as those who consistently do the right thing. They are not a small group of super-saints that have achieved a level of moral perfection so lofty that we have to declare them righteousness (sinless). Over against that unreal expectation, the righteous are those who consistently do the right thing. In the other category are the wicked, those who consistently choose the more nefarious and shocking alternatives. They could be those who live a corrupt and scandalous life, or the more genteel who display the polite forms of wickedness such as greed, envy, and ill-will. In either case the future is not bright. While the categories are clear-cut there are degrees of righteousness as well as degrees of sinfulness.

Solomon turns first to those who have decided to live in a way that is pleasing to the Lord. They are committed to making right choices. Every ethical decision is a chance to say by what you do that God's way is best. Not only at the end of one's life journey but all along the way the result of that mind-set is sheer unadulterated joy. One dictionary defines joy as "the emotion of great delight or happiness caused by something exceptionally good or satisfying." That comes close, but even then when we try to define it, it seems to diminish the true experience. I find that joy sneaks up undetected. It can't be scheduled it can only be experienced when it happens. The joy of the Lord is pure, uplifting, and deeply satisfying. It is the atmosphere of heaven. We'll be breathing it forever. But there is joy along the way as well for every believer.

As for the wicked, the future holds no rewards. Solomon says that the expectations (the hopes) of the wicked "come to nothing." They don't pan out. This, of course, is for them a great disappointment. While the righteous are blessed with a joyful fulfillment of their dreams and aspirations, the wicked mourn a life contrary to the will of God. How good of God to guide us in a way that is pleasant for the present and will ultimately break out in eternal joy. That is not true for the wicked. For them life turns out to be nothing but preparation for eternal disappointment. Solomon, you've done it again! We'd like to sing, so how about, "Praise Gods from whom all blessing flow." It is time for us to lay hold of the joy that not only awaits us but is ever present. In one of his oft-quoted remarks C. S. Lewis chides the weakness of our desires, writing, "We are half-hearted creatures, fooling about with drink and sex and ambition when infinite joy is offered us . . . We are far too easily pleased."

Thirty-five
Humility, the door to wisdom

"Close behind pride comes disgrace, but humility is followed by wisdom" (Proverbs 11:2).

There is a certain dependable sequence in the affairs of life. One thing follows another only to be repeated. Solomon gives two examples, the first being disgrace, which is followed by humility. To elevate oneself leads inevitably to a collapse that displays the illegitimacy of the claim. In life we are who we are, not something more skilled, more profound, more able than we are. It is pride that makes such bold claims. It is quite exhilarating because the prospect of prominence of any sort appeals to our nature. Pride is the universal idiosyncrasy. C. S. Lewis correctly observed that "a proud man is always looking down on things and people; and, of course, as long as you are looking down, you cannot see something that is above you."

The disgrace that follows pride is a stigma not easily overcome. We forgive the ill-informed and even praise the one who tries but fails to achieve, but we hold those unmasked by reality to be culprits of the worst sort. Very few tears for the fall of the proud.

It's a different story with the humble, those rare individuals who have achieved but don't say a word about it. I have a friend living in another state whom I have considered very close for a number of years. Why he never told me he had an airplane I will never know. The subject apparently never came up and he chose not to bring it up. Since flying is part of my background, I was stunned when I learned this bit about him.

The point that Solomon is making is that as disgrace follows pride, so does wisdom follow humility. I understand this to illustrate the truth that wisdom is available for those who approach life with a certain openness and humility. While pride, by definition, is full of itself and therefore has no room for wisdom, humility comes looking for instruction and insights. To be full of oneself leaves little room for the richness and fullness of wisdom.

The lesson is clear: If you take the "high" road of pride, in your fall you'll see humility seated where you thought you'd be. Take the "low" road and you'll find yourself above enjoying the rich benefits of wisdom.

Thirty-six
The vital role of integrity

"The upright are guided by their integrity, but the crooked are

destroyed by their duplicity" (Proverbs 11:3).

For people to live responsibly there is one thing that has to be established and that is the question of absolutes: do they exist or not? Are some things right or wrong or do those terms simply reflect how the community feels about an issue? Traditionally, America has governed itself on the basis of the Judeo-Christian world-view that honors life and holds that certain practices will always be wrong regardless of cultural setting. However, ever since the midpoint of last century the American mind has been toying with the possibility of discarding absolutes and enjoying a freedom much like that of Adam in the garden who could eat of any tree except the one in the middle.

Of that one God said, "You must not touch it, or you will die" (Gen. 3:3). Adam's decision to disobey opened the door to anarchy.

I stress this point because throughout recorded history, in every group of people there has been a responsibility to do and to say what conforms to a certain standard. I'm not suggesting that it has been observed, but it has been acknowledged. As Solomon says: There are two kinds of people, the upright and the crooked; the first are "guided by their integrity" and the second are "destroyed by their duplicity." Commitment to integrity results in an orderly society that displays an effective and positive manner of living. The direct opposite is duplicity, best defined as speaking or acting in two different ways to different people about the same matter. We call in double-dealing. Such an approach undermines the possibility of people working together on a common cause. In fact, duplicity destroys those who attempt to get ahead by resorting to intentional misrepresentation for personal advantage. The "crooked" that relate to one another in this way need to listen to the wisdom of Solomon. The proverb points out the self-destructive nature of misrepresentation. It is ironic but true that the sinner sets up his own gallows.

Over against the plight of the crooked we have the bright assurance that those who resist the lure of misrepresentation for personal advantage, that is, the upright, will benefit from their fairness and openness in social exchange. Duplicity guides and crookedness destroys. It is built into the world in which we all live.

Thirty-seven
Without guidance it's bound to fail

"For lack of guidance a nation falls, but there is security in many advisers" (Proverbs 11:14).

A nation is like an individual in that it needs to know where it came from, where it is, and where it is going. Perhaps self-awareness is the best way to put it. Show me a successful person and I will show you a person aware of their past, a good understanding of where they are, and a firm conviction about where they want to end up. I love my native America. I read its history and marvel at the insight and fortitude of those who took the problem of Europe in hand, thought together of what should be and then went out and did it. I love the quiet courage of those who risked it all for a new way to live free. We are truly a great nation. How did it all happen?

In brief it can be said that a previous generation took the idea of freedom seriously and gave it all they had. The result is the most free and successful nation in the world. The challenge for us is to follow the trajectory of greatness and maintain our leadership role in global affairs. And how can we do that? What are the necessary ingredients of success?

Part of the answer is in Solomon's warning that should a nation lack guidance it will fall. Of course guidance is constantly being suggested from every political point of view imaginable. Ideologies press hard to play major role in what will be. I can hear the isolationist call for separation at any cost. Then there are the globalists who celebrate the commonality of the human race and see for the future a world community that in spite of its diversity works together for the good of all. And don't forget the militarists who are confident that a yet larger armed force combined with the latest in electronic armament is the only viable path for a safe future.

We have many advisors and I wouldn't necessarily discount the suggestions of any of them, but I would suggest that we don't forget for the future what has worked so well for us in the past. Why not plan ahead by using the past for examples of what to do and also for what not to do. How about taking what has worked so well for yesterday and adjusting it where necessary for a better tomorrow. It is true that we will prosper from "many advisors" but let's be sure that we choose the right ones.

Thirty-eight
Could 20 minus 10 equal . . say, 14?

"Give freely and you will have more; be stingy and you'll lose what you have" (Proverbs 11:24).

On the TV and other places we get a lot of advice about how to be better off financially. In fact, I've seen that one man selling gold so often that he seems like a friend of the family. There are ideas galore about how to have the wealth necessary to own a partnership in some classy beach extravaganza where everyone is younger and it never snows. Sometimes I pray, "Lord, Keep the option open until I can complete the arrangements. The idea behind it all is the strange concept that you get by spending. Our nation with its current 20 trillion dollar debt is proof that it doesn't work. Let's look to Solomon for the moment to see if he is nodding okay.

No, he is saying that is by "giving freely" that we will "have more." Now that's a different approach. It is giving that we receive. Not only that, but if we are "stingy" (hoard everything for ourselves) we will "loose what we have." How could that be? Simple calculation tells me that if I have 20 and give away 10, I will have 10 left, but a recount shows that I still have more than 10. How could that be? The problem with the earlier method of counting is that it leaves God out. It so happens that he is a giver and to encourage us to approach all of life as he does, he blesses those who give and withdraws from those who hoard. I have this picture in my mind of a somewhat playful God who loves to correct not by the application of some severe impersonal law but by letting us experience for the moment what would happen should we decide to follow his lead

Thirty-nine
Doers and Dreamers – Are they
both necessary?

Remind me, Solomon – when was it that you were king of Israel? You say it's been so long ago that it's hard to know for sure but it was probably about 830 B.C. You were in the early twenties when you became king following the death of your father David.

I bring this up because in what we call the book of Proverbs (12:11) you wrote, *"Those who work their land will have abundant food, but those who chase fantasies have no sense."* In the 21st century those of a more conservative outlook would say that this describes accurately the difference between themselves and liberals. "Those who work their land (the conservatives) will have abundant food" but "those who chase fantasies (the liberals) have no sense."

Several things strike me. First, the obvious truth of your statement. Few would deny that genuine commitment to whatever the task may be normally yields a positive reward. That is what almost always happens. And it is also true that "chasing fantasies" is a less secure approach to life. Instead of doing what has proven to work, the person who lives in a sort of dream world is more liable to depend upon others for life's necessities.

However, as with all generalizations, there is always room for the exception. In fact, I would add that the fantasy chaser is a necessary part of a productive society. What happens in the real world begins in the imagination. Technological progress is the result of taking "What if?" seriously. What benefits a society in the long run is to recognize and utilize both mentalities. It is when one assumes center stage and relegates the other to the wings that things go wrong.

So, Solomon, you are absolutely right in identifying the two tendencies. Working has its rewards, dreaming unconnected to reality is not very productive. And isn't it interesting that your observation made about 3,000 years ago is still very true. It would appear that genuine truth is trans-generational.

Forty
Victimized by self-deception

In Proverbs 12:15 Solomon states the somewhat obvious point that "the way of fools seems right to them." When we conjure up in our minds the typical picture of a fool we will probably agree that they really don't understand what they are saying. It doesn't take a body language expert to understand from the look on a fool's face that he is quite pleased with what he is saying. And we reason that since a fool is intellectually challenged it follows that he is probably convinced that there is no incongruence between what he says and reality.

But what about the rest of us? We might even ask, "Does my way seem right to me?" With a few minor exceptions now and then we would probably answer affirmatively. What I am doing right now seems right to me. But self-deception is a far more pervasive factor than most are willing to admit. It is very natural to explain that there was a reason for that questionable act. If blame needs to be assigned, then it was someone else fault. Reassigning blame over a lifetime blinds a person to personal responsibility. Character erodes and habit takes control.

Self-deception is the inevitable result of continually lying to oneself. The slight personal benefit of evading personal responsibility carries its own penalty. In time it leaves us unable to think clearly about life. We become victimized by our own refusal to honor truth. Self-justification belongs to "the way of fools" and at what time a person qualifies for that title is hard to pinpoint.

Forty-one
Handling the gift of communication?

Communication is one of God's most precious gifts to mankind. And the tongue can either separate or bring together. Verse 18 of Proverbs 12 speaks of two kinds of people — the "reckless" and the "wise." The former uses the gift of communication to destroy and the latter to heal. It all depends on the tongue. Yet it goes deeper because the tongue is simply the agent in communication for two types of people. The first destroys relationship and the second nurtures it. May those of us touched by the grace of God be wise in speech so a world so ravaged by sin will be, at least to some degree, healed.

Forty-two
Do you speak anthropomorphically?

In your book of Proverbs, Solomon, you say that God "detests lying lips" but "delights" when our speech is "trustworthy" (12:22). In the twenty-first century that falls strange on our ears. We tend to think of God as above all the reactions that are common to man. But you say that when we lie, God actually reacts negatively, he detests our "lying lips." Conversely he experiences delight when what we say can be trusted. How do you explain that?

SOLOMON: Well, to speak at all of God is to think and speak from within the perspective of limited human beings. When he communicates to the angelic host I haven't the faintest idea how he goes about it but when he has something to say to us his only option is to use our language and our thought forms. When we speak of God we speak anthropomorphically, that is, we speak of him as through he were a human being. So when I write that God "takes delight" I am describing his reaction as though he were man.

I think I understand. To say that God is reacting emotionally exactly as we do is to assign to the words an unintended literalism. However at the same time, we should not diminish the emotional impact of the words because obviously God doesn't react exactly like we do.

SOLOMON: Exactly right. The best we can do is to use descriptive words as the best way to represent God as actually detesting lying but delighting in truth. Precisely what is happening within the emotional structure of God is simply beyond our grasp. It is enough to know that he both "detests" and "delights."

Forty-three
The problem of the tongue

"The prudent keep their knowledge to themselves, but a fool's heart blurts out folly" (Proverbs 12:23)

Would Solomon have us understand that those who are wise should not share with others the information that they've gained either by insight or experimentation? By no means. We all recognize the significant contributions made by the "wise" that have made western civilization the global model. If the wise did not "speak" the welfare of civilization would be serioiusly damaged. Michael Faraday's work in the field of electromagnetism opened the way to the development of the electric motor. Had he "kept this to himself" we would all be the losers.

So who is Solomon speaking about? Context suggests that the warning not to speak is directed at those who are apt to open their mouth whenever the opportunity arises. To speak when there is nothing to say is more likely the result of a person's desire to be noticed. It is an ego problem. So often what purports to be a discussion is nothing but a series of "overlapping monologues." Prudent people do not allow themselves to be trapped into that sort of exchange. It is the fool whose "heart blurts out folly."

It appears that the fool is a major topic of the book of Proverbs. A quick count shows that the designation occurs 72 times in the 31 chapters. Solomon counsels wisdom over folly and in the verse under discussion we learn of a major distinctive of the fool — the necessity to speak even though no one is interested. "Blurting out folly" puts the speaker into a very unsavory category. So next time we are tempted to speak it might be a good idea to ask ourself why. Do we want to convey information or simply impress? Better a wise man unheard than a fool with a microphone.

Forty-four
Excessive talking is narcissism on display

In his Book of Proverbs, King Solomon observed, "Those who guard their lips preserve their lives" (13:3). Do we need yet another warning about loose lips? Apparently so, because while many of us have been told from youth not to talk so much, we still find ourselves unable to simply be quiet.

Why do people talk on and on when no one is listening? Usually that sort of chatter is not intended to inform but to demonstrate how much one knows about any and every subject. Face it – excessive talking is narcissism on display. Solomon believed that the talker doesn't "preserve his life" because in telling all he knows he exposes all his weaknesses. I had an acquaintance once that was not at all a talker, but he normally showed up at every function immaculately dressed and looking like the go-to person. I used to marvel at the gentle knowing smile that covered his face while others were arguing a point. He was "Chancey Gardiner" redux for sure. He simply didn't talk in public. He didn't have to because his rather naïve attitude was convincing evidence of his wise grasp of the subject.

One of the rare graces of life is to withhold comment whenever it adds nothing to the conversation. Besides, it is clear that learning goes into neutral when the mouth is engaged. Thank you Solomon for the reminder.

Forty-five
Wounded pride results in strife

One sign of an inquiring mind is its continuing search for the cause that underlies the problem. It's not enough simply to offer an answer that is on the same level. We can't solve A by replacing it with B; what is required is the reason for A. So when Solomon says, "*Where there is strife there is pride*" (13:10) he wants us to understand that the real culprit is not the strife but its underlying cause – pride.

Strife is the result of a bruised ego. Should you question the superiority of my point of view you have assaulted not only what I think but, more importantly, who I believe myself to be. Pride is wounded and strife is the result.

What complicates the problem in society is that is that self-regard is universal. By nature we are all descendants of the primal pair who bought into Satan's lie that God was withholding from them something of value. They were offended by that single restriction ("Not that tree!") and pride was born. Pride now expresses itself in life by any number of sins, one of which is strife.

So the answer to the problem of strife is not benevolent disregard or perhaps renewed opposition but a clear understanding that all such surface problems can be remedied only by a renewal of the inner man. Outward change inevitably depends on inward transformation.

Forty-six
To scorn instruction carries a price

"Whoever scorns instruction will pay for it, but whoever respects a command is rewarded" (Proverbs 13:13).

It is interesting that life has a sort of built-in reward/penalty system. Do something right and you are rewarded; do it wrong and nothing turns out as expected. However there seem to be a lot of exceptions; for example, unfair business people make huge profits and scrupulously honest people go bankrupt.

So it seems, but the picture changes when one's perspective broadens to include eternity. In the Psalms, David often laments the material successes of the wicked but then remembers that life here on earth is not the entire story.

The point that Solomon is making is that one's reaction to instruction or command has consequences. Should pride lead us to feel that in a given situation we know it all or that we are under no obligation to conform to authority of truth, then we will suffer the consequences. The converse is equally true. Admit our limited grasp of the subject and conform to its normal requirements and we are rewarded.

But what if on a given subject we are in fact thoroughly informed? There's another problem: the notion that we can know all that can be known about a subject. Wisdom teaches that the more we know the more we understand how little we know. So remain open to instruction and respect the insight of others. It will guide you on your journey to truth and reward you along the way.

Forty-seven
We do what we think

"Good judgment wins favor, but the way of the unfaithful leads to their destruction" (Proverbs 13:15).

When studying the wisdom literature of the Old Testament it is important to pay attention to the structure of the psalm or proverb. Looking at Proverbs 13:15 we can see an A-B-A-B structure: "Good judgment" leads to "favor" as "the way of the faithful" leads to "destruction." So what can learn from this?

Favor and destruction are clearly opposites. One kind of living brings God's approval while the other his condemnation. On the other hand, while good judgment (or "keen insight" as the NLT has it) is a static quality, "the way of the unfaithful" suggests a course of action. Our conduct is not simply a series of independent actions but the result of a basic mindset.

We talk about spontaneous reactions. A car suddenly appears from nowhere at a breakneck speed and before we can "think it through" we have jammed on the brakes. That reaction was the result of years of subconscious conditioning. In the same way, good judgment in the world of moral decisions enjoys the favor of God and doesn't allow us to pursue a way of living that ends up in destruction. We might say, "Blessed is the man whose spontaneous reaction to a sudden moral crisis comes from a heart conditioned by years of obedience to God." Of course, you, Solomon, would have a more pithy way to put it. Perhaps something like "Wisdom prevents wreckage."

Forty-eight
The experiential nature of wisdom

"Walk with the wise and become wise, for a companion of fools suffers harm" (Proverbs 13:20).

To "walk with the wise" is to share their companionship and allow what they know to become part of one's own approach to life. By gradually adopting their way of looking at life we become wise, and that wisdom is not something we acquired by applying the rules of logic to a body of facts. Wisdom and knowledge are related but are not one and the same. Knowledge is the sum total of accumulated facts while wisdom is the insight that allows us to see how they apply to life. Knowledge is fact based, wisdom is experiential and relational.

So if you desire wisdom, choose as companions the wise. Fools may appear to make the moment a bit more fun but should you buy into that approach you will pay a price for it.

Forty-nine
Failure to discipline is a hostile act

"Those who spare the rod of discipline hate their children. Those who love their children care enough to discipline them" (Proverbs 13:24 NLT).

One of life's most important lessons is that actions have

consequences. Nothing in life can be done apart from its corresponding result. We do not live in a moral vacuum. Solomon is telling us that if we truly love our children we will discipline them.

There was a time when appropriate discipline was expected both by the child as well as society at large. With the passage of time the proverbial "rod" has been set-aside on the shelf of enlightened parenting. Even mild application of the rod has for the most part been replaced with some form of correction less physical.

For the moment, let's accept the position that we are not to take "rod" in a literal sense, but that it carries the idea of withholding something that the child desires. They are required to "sit in the corner" for a time, or be denied access to the family car, or be required to make amends for their wrong. The point remains the same; if a parent fails to discipline a child, they have deprived the child of the correction necessary to arrive safely at responsible adulthood – and that is to "hate" them. While the failure of parents to discipline relieves them of that unpleasant task, it places the inevitable consequences of unacceptable behavior on the child. Not to correct may at the moment seem like a loving act, but Solomon names it for what it is.

To restate the proverb as a question we could ask, "Do we love our children enough to discipline them?" Failure in this crucial obligation is hostility toward the child.

Fifty
It isn't right because it seems to be

"*There is a way that appears to be right, but in the end it leads to death*" (Proverbs 14:12).

What is it that makes a course of action appear to be right? Well, it could be the result of careful analysis of the issue but all too often it is no more than a quick emotional response. It simply seems to be right. I believe Solomon is warning us that there are issues in life of such importance that it is not enough simply to **feel** that something is right but that the issue calls for serious attention. Certainly life is one of those issues.

Just because something appears to be right it doesn't necessarily follow that it is right. One of the debilitating effects of our fallen nature is that we are prone to self-deception. It all began in the Garden of Eden when the first couple decided that their view of the fruit on that one tree was superior to God's. Ever since that tragic decision we have been inclined to evaluate everything in terms of how we think it is or should be. Called self-deception. No wonder that there is a certain way of looking at life that "appears to be right." It may well appear to be that way because we have decided that it is, not because it is. The "way" that Solomon is questioning is the way of man apart from God. The problem is that from man's limited perspective one cannot see the issue in its entirety. Lots of things appear to be desirable if we can't or won't consider the outcome. God knows the result of every possible course of action so it is wise for us who are limited by nature to pay attention.

Solomon wants us to understand that the path of life that appears to be right to those living apart from God is in fact the road to death. Since we are dealing with issues of life and death should we not listen to God?

Fifty-one
Who does Solomon mention so often?

"The wise fear the Lord and shun evil, but a fool is hotheaded and yet feels secure" (Proverbs 14:16)

Since wisdom is the major topic of Proverbs it's no surprise that the fool is mentioned 37 times in the one book. These references tell us a number of things about fools — that they deny the existence of God (14:1), find pleasure in scheming (10:23), spurn discipline (15:5), are quick to quarrel (20:3), and a number of other similar qualities. Our proverb for today tells us that the fool is hotheaded *"yet feels secure."* In spite of the fact that they are easily provoked and volatile they are unaware of any risk connected with that questionable attitude.

We all need to be careful not to allow how we feel about something to be the ultimate judge of whether it is right or wrong. What the fool has done is to create his own moral universe. Self-deception has played a major role in his decisions and brought him to the place where an act is wrong only if it upsets his own moral balance. He may approve of an action considered wrong by others because to him it seems okay; one example being his own hotheaded approach to life.

By contrast, the wise "fear (that is, "stand in awe of") the Lord and shun evil." Their guide to what is right or wrong is not how they feel about it about it but whether or not it is consistent with the nature of God as revealed in Scripture. Unlike the fool, the Christian has surrendered his own fallible judgment to the expressed will of God.

Fifty-two
Getting rich by giving away

"The poor are shunned even by their neighbors, but the rich have many friends" (Proverbs 14:20).

Unfortunately that is absolutely true. We see disadvantaged on television and are grateful that God has helped us secure a better station in life. An actual visit to the poorer section of any city in America is an experience that leaves a lasting impression.

Then there are the rich. Solomon tells us that they *"have many friends,"* but I sense a bit of satire here. So often those who flock to the rich are drawn not by a genuine sense of friendship, but because of the personal benefit they may gain from the association. That sort of "friendship" is highly suspect. Friendship is the selfless act of always being available for the enrichment of the other, not a calculated maneuver to associate with those who have for personal benefit. The narcissism involved in securing profitable relationships under the guise of friendship is the direct opposite of true friendship.

I suspect that should those who expend energy in order to benefit from the rich would redirect that energy toward finding ways to alleviate the plight of the poor, they would suddenly discover the real difference between genuine friendship and the fraudulent brand they were engaged it. A central truth of the Christian faith is that by serving the interests of the other we find ourselves on the sure path to personal fulfillment. Human nature would have us direct our time and energy toward that which is of personal benefit but the answer lies 180 degrees in the opposite direction. It is by being a friend that we receive all the rich benefits of friendship.

Fifty-three
Why this world needs both talkers and givers

"All hard work brings a profit, but mere talk leads only to poverty" (Proverbs 14:23).

Every social group seems to consist of two kinds of people, the *talkers* and the *workers*. The former live in the land of "what if" and the latter in the land of "what is." Although Solomon sets one over against the other – and his point is certainly valid – it is my contention that by taking the terms in a slightly different sense, we will find that both are necessary. In a perfect world visionaries would think about what could be and workers would make it happen.

A quick look at life, however, convinces us that talking is easier than working – at least the talking that is headed nowhere. And since talking is easier, that is why societies tend to make that choice. At the same time, talking – understood as careful consideration of life's difficulties with the desire to find a profitable solution – is both demanding and beneficial. It would be accurate to call that kind of talking "work."

When we apply this distinction to political life, talkers tend to be liberal and workers conservative. Unfortunately each questions whether the other is all that important. However if there were only "liberals," a nation could well find itself pursuing goals that, while idealistically desirable, would be practically impossible. (Which reminds me of a story from WW 2 about a liberal's solution for the threat of German submarines – "Empty the oceans." When asked, "How?" the conservative was told, "That's your problem.") On the other hand, if a society had no liberals there could well be a fatal lack of attention to newer methods of achieving traditional goals.

It is interesting, is it not, how words take on the meaning ascribed to them. If we take Solomon's "mere talk" in the sense of openness to what could be, and couple it with "hard work" then we have the best of both worlds. Now that's a subject that calls for some serious talking, or should we say "work?"

Fifty-four
What does it mean to do the right thing?

"Righteousness exalts a nation, but sin condemns any people" (Proverbs 14:34).

It is customary to think of righteousness in the abstract as if it were a quality that a person can possess. But righteousness is not something that you have but something that you do. A person's righteousness is not a philosophical construct, but the result of always doing the right thing.

Solomon is telling us two things about living this way. First, that always choosing to do the right thing "exalts a nation," or as several other translations have it, "makes a nation great." National greatness is not something assigned to a nation because of its outstanding record in such things as growth, financial stability, or global prominence, but the result of making principled moral choices. It is at this point where our own nation has to ask itself whether it can be considered a "righteous" nation if it allows the selling of baby parts, uses government agencies to punish those who disagree, or ignores corruption in finance and business.

The contrast to making the right moral choices is to sin. Doing the wrong thing "condemns any people." We live in a moral universe and there is no way for a person or a nation to continue doing wrong and escape condemnation. It's part of the package. By our conduct we determine our own future – greatness or disgrace. And that is true at every level.

Well Solomon, you were known as the wisest man of your time, but it is helpful to know that what you are saying is supported by common sense as well as by informed discussion.

Fifty-five
The power of gentleness

"A gentle answer turns away wrath, but a harsh word stirs up anger" (Proverbs 15:1).

That harsh words stir up anger is easy to understand. No one likes to be verbally assaulted. Depending on one's temperament the reaction to harsh words runs all the way from silent resentment to something a lot more obvious, but in either case it is some form of anger. Whether or not one's response is justified is a separate issue. The point here is that harsh words inevitably stir up some form of animosity. Should one ask whether harsh words have accomplished something positive the answer would be No. Anger rarely does.

But what if the person answers with gentleness? Now that is quite a different story. While harshness elicits anger, gentleness has a way of diminishing it ("quiets anger" is how the TEV translates it). A gentle answer has a way of defusing the rising conflict. Gentleness is not a weakness but a strength. It shows that a person is able to control his own most powerful adversary, the need to justify oneself. When a person has himself under control he is able to think clearly and answer in a helpful way. Jesus said only two things about himself: that he was "gentle" and that he was "humble in heart" (Matt 11.29). So since as believers we are called to be Christ-like, gentleness is

no longer an option but a divine
expectation.

Fifty-six
What is it that God's detests?

*"The LORD detests the sacrifice
of the wicked, but the prayer of the
upright pleases him"* (Proverbs 15:8).

"It is a bit difficult to think of
God "detesting" something. We can
picture him being pleased but
somehow the opposite seems out of
place. It's not like God. Well,
Solomon, help me understand what
you are saying in Proverbs 15:8 where
you write that Gods detests *"the
sacrifice of the wicked."*

"I know that in the Old Testament a sacrifice was a religious ceremony in which an animal, such as a lamb or a young bull, was killed and its blood presented to God as an offering. Certainly there is nothing wrong with carrying out a religious practice given by God. So why do you say that God "*detests*" the practice?

SOLOMON: God hated it because the wicked people who were carrying it out pretended to be honoring God. What was wrong was the condition of their hearts. That's what changed a beautiful ceremony from being acceptable to eliciting such a powerful reaction from God.

"Then am I correct in assuming that a contemporary parallel would be "playing church" by those whose hearts have never really been changed by the work of God's Holy Spirit? In other words, is it the hypocrisy of insincere religious activity that God hates? Looks like he detests all religious activity that is not genuine."

SOLOMON: You're right. But note that the rest of my proverb goes on to say that "*the prayer of the righteous pleases him.*" We don't worship a cranky old deity who spends his days correcting us for everything we do.

"Apparently, then, it would be better to be bold and bad than to be religious but phony. Thanks for your insight.

Fifty-seven
How to have a cheerful face

"A happy heart makes the face cheerful, but heartache crushes the spirit" (Proverbs 15:3).

Solomon, I've always understood that you were the wisest man of your time. That was about 3,000 years ago, if my calculation is correct. So when I started to read the Book of Proverbs (the best of your thinking saved for posterity) I expected to find a large body of knowledge that in your day was at the cutting edge of thought. But what I discovered was not information but insights. You weren't toying with the remote possibility of something like what we now call space travel or explaining what we now recognize as quantum physics. What God gave you was not knowledge but wisdom. We often say that wisdom is knowledge applied to life and it is for that reason that what you have written is so helpful for living a life that's both satisfying and productive.

(Incidentally, some day I'll ask you to explain how a <u>wise</u> man could have "700 wives and 300 concubines!" 1 Kings 11:3).

In chapter 15 verse 13, you announce the pleasant news that "a happy heart makes the face cheerful." Some one commenting on the state of too many professing believers suggested, "Christians ought to tell their face that they love Jesus." I'm convinced that there are a good number of secular people who would take the Christian faith more seriously if they saw on the faces of its adherents some reflection of the deep joy of sins forgiven and the buoyant expectation of life eternal. We could all benefit from taking with all seriousness the lines from Psalm 100 in the Scottish Psalter: "Sing to the Lord with cheerful voice, Him serve with mirth, his praise forth tell." I especially like the idea of serving God "with mirth." Improper, you say? Well, only in church perhaps, but never when enjoying His presence.

The flip side of the "happy heart" is the "heartache," and that "crushes the spirit." That life provides a number of those tragic experiences cannot be denied and there are times to mourn, but in all the other times let's not pretend that living with Jesus is a downer. Cheer up, the best is not only yet to come, but for the most part is already here.

Fifty-eight
Cheerfulness is a choice not a condition

"All the days of the oppressed are wretched, but the cheerful heart has a continual feast" (Proverbs 15:15).

If by the term "the oppressed" you are referring to the poor, those who are financially destitute and socially ostracized, you are certainly right in describing their lot in life as "wretched." A quick trip through an underprivileged neighborhood will convince anyone of that. The TEV translates the verse, "The life of the poor is a constant struggle." However I think the term has a wider reference to anyone who is tyrannized by some powerful influence over which they cannot break free. There are nations that hold their people in check with autocratic systems operating for the good not of the people but for the ruling few. That also is "wretched."

Over against this rather dark background Solomon tells us about another class of people, those with a "cheerful heart." While there may be some overlapping of categories, by and large they represent two distinct groups. It is not that adequate resources produce a happy heart, although we all recognize that cheerfulness is far more likely to be found where the financial burdens of life are less pressing. However, the point that Solomon is making is that having a cheerful heart is an unconditional celebration that goes on and on. It is a "continual feast."

I believe that cheerfulness is a choice. While a stressful situation makes it more difficult, it is still a choice that you make. To choose a somewhat sad and overly serious mindset for life is to go to bat with two strikes against you. The decision to be cheerful, in contrast to waiting for something to make us that way, reflects a character much to be desired. Optimism, geniality, buoyancy, cheerfulness – or however you would put it – is not only a gift to others but to ourselves as well. As the NJB puts it, "for the joyous heart it is always festival time."

Fifty-nine
Is it frightening to fear the Lord?

"Wisdom's instruction is to fear the Lord, and humility comes before honor" (Proverbs 15:33).

One thing I have noticed about your style of writing, Solomon, is that your choice of words allows a certain freedom in translation. For example, the NIV says that "Wisdom's instruction" is to fear the Lord while the TEV says that the fear of the Lord is "an education in itself." Differences like these demonstrate that words are not fixed units of meaning but, as the linguist Eugene Nida insisted, they "bleed their meaning from context."

Another interesting thing about the verse is the relationship between the two clauses. The first tells us that it is wise to "fear the Lord" and the second that "humility comes before honor." Since there is normally a certain relationship between clauses in Semitic poetry, it would appear that fearing the Lord has an important connection with humility. Let's think about that.

To fear the Lord is not to be afraid of him (as we normally use the word fear) but to be actively aware of his awesome nature. When we are aware of who God really is we are overwhelmed with a feeling of his greatness and absolute perfection. So what is the inevitable response? We are humbled. Having gone to our knees, we confess how incredibly short of his exalted state we fall. It is a genuinely humbling experience to be granted the privilege of being in God's presence.

You've told us, Solomon, that "before you can ever receive honors" (TEV) – and that is what we seem to want so desperately – we "must be humble." So wisdom teaches us to fear the Lord (ascribe to him the perfection revealed in scripture) and we will be humbled and that, in turn, will lead to what we really wanted in the beginning – honor. But this honor is "gained" in a way that removes all desire for personal recognition. Solomon, you certainly have a way of making your point.

Sixty
Is God more concerned with what or with why?

"All a person's ways seem pure to them, but motives are weighed by the Lord." (Proverbs 16:2).

Before commenting on Solomon's proverb I would like to restate a couple of phrases to bring out more clearly what I think the original text had in mind. Let's change "seems pure" to "may seem right" and "weighed by" to "evaluated." Now we have: "Everything a person does may seem right to them, but the Lord evaluates their motives." You might ask, "Why are you changing the sacred text?" and the answer is that I am not. Words must always be understood in context. Very few people would hold that everything they did was "pure." And for God to "weigh" something reflects the ancient practice of measuring grain on a balance scale. It is clearer today to understand God as "evaluating" motives than "weighing" them.

The central issue is the difference in how God and man look at the issues of life. Normally, most people tend to think that whatever they happen to be doing is okay. And everyone is willing to confess a few misdemeanors along the way. God, however, is concerned with why they do what they are doing. He is concerned with motivation. Acts are, by definition, a result not a cause. We do something because we are motivated to do it, not the other way around.

Since we live in a moral universe, the "whats" of life are of less importance than the "whys." Fixation on the act rarely changes anything.

Example: If we continue to expend our energy on correcting a socially unacceptable action it is doubtful that we will ever be able to change it. A far better approach is to examine why a person or group of people do what they do. It is always more useful to consider why.

One other thing about the proverb is its insight into self-deception ("All a person's ways" seem pure to them.") Self-deception is the one weakness for which there seems to be no cure. The blame for everything falls automatically on the other person. Some one noted that in prison it is hard to find any prisoners who believe they are guilty. Whatever the misfeasance, the inmate, in his own eyes, is not guilty. Someone else is at fault. Or, whatever the nature of a church split, it is "those other people" who are at fault. The inability to see one's own role in a fractured relationship is the normal result of an inborn narcissism. Confession and continual awareness both of the problem and of God's provision for the humble is the only answer.

Sixty-one
When would having less be better?

"Better a little with righteousness than much gain with injustice" (Proverbs 16:8).

Some things are simply better than other things. We go through life making decisions and we choose by nature whatever seems to us to be better in a given situation. And how do we decide that A is better than B? A major factor in every decision is how we think it will affect us personally; how will it serve our interests. Of course there are other reasons why we should choose A over B but self-concern seems to be the critical factor in every decision.

The Christian faith understands this dominant concern for self as the historic result of a decision in the Garden of Eden. The primal pair decided to disobey God. In any case, it is not difficult for the reflective mind to recognize the universal nature of narcissism. The result is that our judgment of the right course of action is normally determined by our view of how that decision will affect us personally. What we need for good decision-making is advice from one who is not affected by this malady. That, of course, brings us to God.

So, Solomon, in the proverb we are discussing you say that "a little with righteousness" is better than "much gain with injustice." We might put the question this way: When it comes to having stuff, is it better to have more or less? Is the minimalist right in holding that having too much blocks our way to a satisfying life, or the maximalist who would say that having more is always better?

SOLOMON: Your questions are interesting but you've have missed the point I was making. It is not how much you have but the way you get it that is the important issue. One might think that "much gain" is better but if you got it in a way that was unfair, then compared to the person who has very little but earned it fairly, you are the looser. Better a somewhat meager life if you are playing the game fairly than to be in the top 5% if the way to the top was unfair. To have is not the goal of life and things themselves are of value only when they are used for a more noble purpose.

Sixty-two
Would you rather have wisdom than gold?

"How much better to get wisdom than gold, to get insight rather than silver!" (Proverbs 16:16).

Decisions, decision! It seems like if we aren't deciding where, then the question is how, or what, or why, or

when, or which. We know that some
ways to accomplish a task are simply
better than others. Some decisions
lead to a better result. Solomon's
proverbs deal with what we might call
"the better choice," or, more simply
"wisdom." That is what wisdom is –
making the better choice in each of
the many decisions we face every day.

Few would argue against the
value of gold and silver. It enables us
to accomplish with ease the normal
concerns of life: purchasing the house
we want, paying the merchant for
what we need for sustenance, making
provision for a pleasant retirement,
etc. But what our proverb states is that
there are a couple of things that are
better than being able to buy all we
need for a comfortable existence:
"wisdom" is better than gold, and
"insight" is better than silver.

We probably already knew that . . . but, did we? We know, for instance, that a certain habit may have serious consequences, but we continue to indulge ourselves in it. I would hold that in a case like that we don't know it. To really know something is to act accordingly. I'm afraid that as a society we don't know, in the sense of acting on it, that wisdom is better than gold. The pursuit of gold, understood as accruing money and things as the basis for "the good life," is the determining factor in the lives of most.

So why is wisdom better? The answer is that it directs us to a way of living that is far more satisfying than any alternative. The practical problem at this point is how to recognize the better alternative. An informed reflection on life will be helpful, but beyond that, for the Christian believer, there is the wisdom of God laid out clearly in sacred scripture. So far in life I've found that his way has always proven superior to what I would have chosen on my own. The wise thing to do is to listen to the Author of Life himself.

Sixty-three
Deceived by a limited understanding

"There is a way that appears to be right, but in the end it leads to death" (Proverbs 16:25).

There is one thing about time that can't be denied and that is that it never stops. We are not given the privilege of stepping outside, even for a moment, to get our bearings before we move ahead. In our proverb for today we find ourselves on a "way," a path or road leading us from this particular moment in time on into the future. Solomon speaks about a certain way "that appears to be right" and, if I understand him correctly, the way he refers to is the way that excludes God. Adam and Eve, following their act of disobedience, were put out of the garden, leaving God behind. They were on their own and blinded by sin, so it is easy to understand why the path they chose "appeared [to them] to be right."

The essential point is that mankind, blinded by sin, is unable to discern the outcome of life apart from God. We are deceived by our own limited understanding of reality. We may think that life apart from God is the way to go but that doesn't make it so. Solomon makes it clear that that way of living leads to death.

But what kind of death are we talking about? Certainly not physical death. We all die apart from how we may have lived. So far only one person has returned from death and that was Jesus whose resurrection is the logical reason for accepting as true what he taught about life and eternity. The death that Solomon is speaking about is death as eternal separation from God. Since God is life, his absence is death. The most graphic picture of hell is the eternal loneliness of separation from the only true source of joy and personal fulfillment.

I know that this is a stern proverb. It focuses on the darker side of existence. The good news is that there is another way and that way leads to life – not only eternal life, but real life in the here and now. As John the evangelist put it, speaking for Jesus, "I am come that they might have life, and that they might have it more abundantly" (10:10).

Sixty-four
The perverse influence of gossip

"A perverse person stirs up conflict, and a gossip separates close friends" (Proverbs 16:28).

Since the English word "perverse" has some strange connotations. It will be well to note that the underlying Hebrew text is better understood as "a man of falsehoods, a liar," and the "gossip," more precisely, as "one who whispers and murmurs." One thing for sure is that people like that do "*stir up conflict*" and even "*separate close friends.*"

It is clear that generally speaking conflict does not move a society toward desirable goals. Once an acceptable pattern for a healthy society has been determined then what is required for success is the full cooperation of all the people. The only role for "conflict" along the way is when in times of review people are reassessing goals and planning how to achieve them. What Solomon is addressing is the questionable practice of people who for personal reasons are setting others at odds. In that case division in the group serves their personal agenda. Perhaps "perverse" is not a bad translation after all.

The parallel offense is gossip, that rather insidious tendency to share information or rumor that would be better left unsaid. I can't imagine anyone arguing on behalf of gossip yet I know of no other trait so universally shared. It's not whether something is right or wrong that determines whether it should be shared, but whether sharing it would be beneficial for all involved. However in that case it could not be labeled gossip.

Once again Solomon has told us what we already know. No one could argue with a straight face that practices such as misrepresentation or betraying confidentiality are beneficial. Yet, the importance of always doing the right thing is a lesson that probably needs to be learned on a continuing basis.

Sixty-five
Who's in charge?

"The lot is cast into the lap, but its every decision is from the LORD" (Proverbs 16:33).

Cleromancy was the practice of divination by casting lots. The practice was widely used in ancient times and often occurs both in the Old Testament (some 70 times) and in the New Testament as well (for instance, in Matt. 27:35 the Romans soldiers divided up Jesus' clothes by casting lots.) Even today we flip a coin to determine everything from making a tough decision to deciding which football team gets to choose to kick or receive. So Solomon says that while "we may throw the dice" it is the Lord who "determines how they fall" (as the NLT phrases it).

The point of the proverb is that God is in charge of everything so that even the decisions we make are determined by him. The question being answered is, "Who is in charge." From the secular point of view the idea that God might be involved in our everyday decisions in life (at least those big enough to occasion the flipping of a coin) is bit ludicrous. One might say that "God – if there be one – is certainly too busy for that type of thing." But Judeo-Christian thought has always supported the concept of God's sovereignty. Nothing is left to chance, he is in control. There are almost 700 references in the bible to God's sovereignty. So when the lot is cast it is under the control of God who has already determined how it will fall. Some think that the Urim and the Thummin refer to colored stones in the breastplate of the High Priest used to determine God's will.

The issue of who is in charge in decision-making is not a theological issue for most of contemporary society. We decide. I am the one who decides which car to buy, which route to take, what time we will leave. Of course Solomon wouldn't go along with that. We may cast the dice but we have no control of how they land. Then who does? Is it all at random? Is no one in charge? Of course that sounds ludicrous in the minor decisions of life but interestingly enough when it comes to major issues many moderns have the strange feeling that perhaps some larger force may be involved.

It comes down to a person's basic perspective on life and reality: is matter all there is or is there perhaps a designer behind it all. No problem for Solomon or for those committed to the trustworthiness of scripture: We throw the dice – God determines how they fall. That God is sovereign brings order out of the chaos of life in today's world.

Sixty-six
Be careful about mocking your
Maker

"Whoever mocks the poor shows contempt for their Maker;

whoever gloats over disaster will not go unpunished" (Proverbs 17:5).

This proverb portrays a person or a group making fun of an individual who has failed in life, at least in so far as failure can be measured by how much a person has. It is relatively easy to look down on those who have less than we have. The secular mind reasons that if the other person had only worked harder – "been smarter in their choices, taken advantage whenever possible, etc." – they wouldn't be in the condition they're in.

The proverb says that those who criticize in this way "show contempt for their Maker." It's as if they walk right up to God and mock him for

having created such a loser.
"Certainly, God, you could have done better than that! Just look at that miserable loser!"

How do these self-declared examples of perfection arrive at this conclusion? Obviously, by trying to measure quality as if it were something material. One cannot make a qualitative judgment on a quantitative basis. Like anyone else, some of the poor may lack integrity but you would never know it by measuring the amount of stuff they have accumulated. There are numerous factors involved in attaining wealth and many of them have nothing to do with what the rich themselves have done. They are givens. And there are many reasons why poverty prevails and many of them are not the fault of the poor.

To mock God by leveling this thoughtless criticism against another is a serious sin. Solomon writes, "*No one who laughs at distress will go unpunished*" (NJB). Just what that punishment will be is not said. However, I would like to conjecture that one such punishment is the deleterious effect of mockery on the mocker himself. By looking down on others we damage ourselves. No one looks forward to being stranded on a desert island with a pathological faultfinder. Of course there will be punishment beyond the self-inflicted damage of criticism, but those judgments are best left with the Lord.

Sixty-seven
The danger of overlooking genre

"A rebuke impresses a discerning person more than a hundred lashes a fool" (Proverbs 17:10).

I imagine that most of us, if pressed for a decision, would claim to be a discerning person. If so, then we are the kind of people who take rebukes very seriously. In fact, a rebuke makes a greater impression on us than would one hundred lashes on the back of a fool. In some of the more graphic cinemas we see the "fool" stripped and being severely beaten with a whip. It takes a long time to get to the hundredth lash! And Solomon wants us to believe that such a brutal ordeal would make less of an impression than would a single rebuke. Does he expect us to believe that?

I've taken the language of the proverb in a very literal fashion in order to highlight something about words. At best, words can give us only a general idea of what the writer wants to communicate. Meaning, to a certain extent, has to be supplied by the reader. That is not to say that readers make up their own meaning but that they understand the words in a context that they have to supply. Meaning is the cooperative result of words and context.

Another thing about language is that more often than not it is best understood somewhat metaphorically. That is obvious when we read in a poem that "mountains clap their hands" or when we say that a certain person is "puffed up." In the first case we recognize that nature is being pictured as having a great time and in the second we don't picture a person being inflated like a big balloon. Common sense takes the words in context and derives meaning from the combination.

So how does this related to the proverb? Since the historic Christian faith takes scripture with all seriousness there is a tendency to take its words in an overly literal fashion. One might even interpret our proverb to mean that a single rebuke hurts a discerning person more than one hundred lashes would with a whip. Since readers ultimately create their own shade of meaning I would argue that it is vitally important to keep in mind the metaphorical nature of so much of language. Don't make a statement to mean what you want it to mean by taking the words in an overly-literal sense.

Sixty-eight
Taking the bullet for a friend

"A friend loves at all times, and a brother is born for a time of adversity" (Proverbs 17:17).

What Solomon is telling us is that a true friend will be loyal no matter what the cost or what the situation. Now that kind of love is a rare commodity in the world, valuable behind measure. Offer me riches or genuine friendship and I'll take the latter. One writer defined friendship as "the inexpressible comfort of feeling safe."

The second clause speaks of a "brother," Some scholars believe this term is to be understood as an alternative for "friend." Others think that friendship will handle most difficult situations, but when real adversity raises its ugly head you need a blood relationship. After thinking about this I came to the conclusion that it doesn't really matter. Infinite delineation is the word game of the intellectual not a realistic approach to problem solving. A friend "loves at all times" (I like the NLT's "always loyal") and a brother, be he family member or just like one, will always be there to help when life has turned rough. You can trust a friend/brother to be there when you need them.

I will always remember a scene in the movie Dave where the White House security agent tells Dave, the presidential double who has been doing so well until it is discovered that the president has really died, that he would "take a bullet for him." And there was no doubt that he would. The authenticity of the agent comes through so clearly that you wouldn't question for a moment that in such a case he would take that fatal step and die for Dave. That is what friends do. They "love at all times," they are "born for a time of adversity."

Sixty-nine
How to get a happy heart

"A cheerful heart is good medicine, but a crushed spirit dries up the bones" (Proverbs 17:22).

Norman Cousins, the famous editor of Saturday Review, was losing his battle with a serious heart disease when he decided that, instead of continuing on the medication that had been assigned to him, he would administer to himself massive doses of Vitamin C and teach himself how to laugh. The latter he did by watching Marx Brothers films. He wrote of his joyous discovery that ten minutes of good belly laughter would give him at least two hours of pain-free sleep. So successful was the "prescription" that not only did he heal himself but he became a professor in the UCLA School of Medicine. Solomon would say to him, "I told you so – a cheerful heart is good medicine."

So who doesn't want to be cheerful? It is sure a lot better than what Solomon calls the "crushed

spirit" which "dries up the bones."
The obvious question is, "How do you
get a cheerful heart?" Life is tough
and full of difficulties that crush the
spirit. Maybe a little bit of cheer now
and then, but by and large life is no
laughing matter. That's where most of
us need a bit of education. The truth is
that happiness or cheer is a decision
that the individual makes. Facts may
set the stage but we make the
decision. We can do that. We can
decide to be cheerful. No one can
stop us.

The common view is that our
reactions are caused by others. It is
what they do that determines how we
feel about it. To agree to that myth is
to place ourselves at the mercy of
others. We become victimized. There
is amply evidence from those working
in the field that we ourselves are those

who decide how to react. Granted, it feels good to be told that it is their fault, not ours, but it is a psychological heresy as well.

So since we are the ones who decide whether or not to have a cheerful heart, let's leave our self-constructed emergency room, take a deep breath and say, I am a cheerful person. Then be that way. Others will like it and your self-esteem will blossom. Talk about win-win!

Seventy

Are your conversations "overlapping monologues"?

"The one who has knowledge uses words with restraint, and whoever has understanding is even-tempered" (Proverbs 17:27).

I am sure that most of us have friends who apparently can't stop talking. We say that such and such a person does not have an unexpressed thought. It just comes naturally. But Solomon says that the wise use words with restraint. They talk, yes, but not more than the occasion requires.

Now before we make a case against excessive verbalization let's remember that proverbs are generalities. We all have a least one good friend who brightens every party with an endless stream of witty remarks. So while it is generally true that wisdom advises us against commenting on everything, there are exceptions.

Why does the informed person restrain his words? One answer may be reflected in the TEV translation: "Those who are sure of themselves do not talk all the time." If I have evidence that supports my point of view I don't need to defend it so vigorously. It's the lack of information that leads to the prolonged defense. That reminds me of what was written in the margin of a certain minister's sermon notes: "Argument weak; Yell like hell!" I've always liked to watch conversations that are aptly described as "overlapping monologues." In fact, I am probably guilty of taking part in more than one of them.

The second clause of the proverb states a parallel truth: "Whoever has understanding is even-tempered." The underlying Hebrew word means "cool of spirit." There is a question whether understanding creates an even temper or whether it is the even temper that leads to understanding. I would think both are true. If I genuinely understand an issue I don't need to go into histrionics to convince someone. Overstatement is for the under-informed.

So what can we learn from this? Certainly, the value of wisdom. It goes without saying that apart from a surprise party it is better to know than not to know. Secondly, that wisdom has a way of eliminating extensive verbiage. To know something is to have gotten to the heart of the issue and that in turn yields to a simpler explanation. Unnecessary explanation is the result of complexity not yet understood.

71027804R00129

Made in the USA
Columbia, SC
18 May 2017